Practical Mayan Astrology

© 2015 – Eric Jackson Perrin
www.coaching-evolution.net

Published by: Eric Jackson Perrin
69300 Caluire et Cuire – France

Printed in Germany by BoD – Books en Demand

ISBN: 979-10-94871-17-1

Legal deposit:October 2015

****

A very warm thank you to

Nieves, Felix, Claudio and Aton
For their teachings

And to all the seekers and masters
who contributed to help recover
Mayan memory, culture and wisdom

***

Books from the same author

The birth Diamond – Sacred numerology – Kindle amazon

The new I Ching – Kindle amazon

****

Summary

<u>Once upon a time...Mayan Astrology !</u>

In Lak'esh Ala K'in! Hi and welcome! Mayan astrology arrived in my life during a hot summer day, in July 2005, in a very nice house built at the foot of a pine covered mountain, on the island of Mallorca, where part of my family is from.

Having practiced western astrology for over 25 years, I did not imagine that day what I was about to discover. It was actually quite a shock. I got the feeling of being in contact with my "essence", as if I entered a tunnel inside me, towards deep down and at the end of which existed keys that I was looking for to make progress. I also remembered something that had been forgotten for a very long time. I was told that Mayan astrology often has such an impact.

Mayan astrology gave me a different vision of space and time as I discovered that Mayan sages have known since a very long time that civilizations emerge, express themselves and then disappear, on planet Earth and also elsewhere, on other planets. It finally helped me become aware of that specific part of a human being that never changes because it is eternal. I then decided to learn, do research and experiment.

Mayan astrology is unusual, surprising and amazing. It seems to come from another time and space where eternity and daily life live side by side. Probably because of its power of truth, it has been for quite a while kept aside and buried in the graves of history and of Spanish conquest, alongside with Mayan culture.

Since a few decades, Maya writing, culture and astrology have been resurfacing thanks to the work and devotion of men and wemen who want to make it live once more and to share it. This very wish made me write this book and share with you what I have discovered and experienced. There are very few books on Mayan astrology. This book is there so that you can acquire strong foundations in calling upon Mayan astrology and to help you make this inner journey towards the center of yourself.

Have a great trip

Best regards
Eric Jackson Perrin 2014.

Introduction

Locating the Mayan civilization within human History

Seventy five thousand years ago, on the Indonesian island of Sumatra, a gigantic volcano created a worldwide climatic disaster. Temperatures got a lot colder. Earth was partly covered by ice and the sea level went down consequently.

Then, twenty two thousand years BC (before the birth of Jesus Christ) and eight thousand years BC, the earth warmed up again and the sea level rose by about 130 meters. A prosperous civilization existing on American seashores almost totally disappeared while different groups of people arrived on the American continent from Russia, Mongolia and China.

From all this emerged, between three thousand five hundred and one thousand five hundred BC, populations that had, from Peru to United States, common physical, cultural and technological characteristics : building of pyramids, cultivating maize, human sacrifices, numerous gods and knowledge of astronomy. Maya is supposed to mean "Maize Man".

The Mayan civilization is very important for several reasons. It is the only civilization, along with its cousin the Aztec civilization, to use a writing system which has now been almost totally decoded, to about 95%, after centuries of research. The Mayans also have an incredible knowledge concerning mathematics, astronomy and the forces that influence the human soul.

It offers a journey inside the flow of time and a different look on human beings, on environmental management and on human history on planet Earth, showing that this history goes much further back in time than most history books tell us and yet that we are now very much concerned and affected by what happened then.

Birth, decline and rebirth of Mayan civilization

Actual archeologists date the beginning of Mayan civilization to about one thousand and six hundred years BC and believe it reached its peak between two hundred and fifty years and seven hundred years AD (after the birth of Jesus Christ). A mathematical number called a constant enables us to convert a Mayan date into our current Christian calendar date. Much research has been undertaken to find the right constant. The most commonly used constant, the GMT constant (584283) dates the beginning of the Mayan calendar to 3114 BC while another constant, the VMR constant (774080), dates it back to 2593 BC!

Between 800 and 1700 AD, Mayan cities were abandoned. Mayan lands were then conquered by the Spaniards and the Mayan civilization almost totally disappeared, surviving in secret in very remote places to the great pressure exerted by the catholic religion.

Mayan people weren't totally identical and the various existing groups liked to show their differences. They were organized into "town-states" where each group had specific linguistic, artistic and cultural specificities. Amongst these groups, the most important ones are the Yukatek Mayas, the Quitché Mayas and the Tcholan Maya. Various factors caused the Mayan civilization to decline, long before the arrival of the Spaniards. Mayan noblemen had many wives and concubines. Their over numerous offsprings spent most of their time making war with one another while the population increased too much and too fast considering available existing resources.

Deforestation and overexploitation of agricultural lands due to excess population eroded the land, leading to a decrease in food production and to famine. Research in climatic changes revealed that in Mexico, between seven hundred and fourteen hundred AD, there was a strong decrease in rainfall and therefore is water resources. Climatic changes, an inadapted management of human and natural resources, numerous human sacrifices and endless wars made people lose confidence in their Gods and leaders and so they left the cities.

Nowadays, Mayan sages are asking humanity to preserve its environment and to handle its natural and human resources wisely. Otherwise, the planet's resources and humanity may just disappear within a few centuries from now and the planet may end up just covered up with dust and sand. But they especially offer highly valuable teachings that allow a person to connect with his or her deep inner truth, to live a life that has a meaning and to experience very high levels of awareness and energy. Such levels of energy allow the most advanced people to leave their physical bodies consciously and thus to "die" in full awareness.

For Mayan sages, spiritual growth is a struggle, an inner struggle that mostly takes place in the invisible worlds, within oneself and in daily life. Such struggle requires being like a warrior and to count on one's own strength and efforts to achieve one's goals. To achieve one's goals, a clear intention and a strong desire to do so must be constantly nourished. The major goal that is sought for is a transfer of one's awareness to the very center of oneself so as to place it into one's spiritual body, which is like a luminous ball made of love and fire that is capable of moving in space and time. It is an inner experience that involves walking along a path with different steps and that involves becoming aware, with one's entire body, of the different bodies that make up a human being down here on Earth.

This requires energy. Important parts of these teachings are becoming aware of the energy flow inside us, increasing one's energy level and saving energy so as to become able to transfer one's ordinary self to one's superior self. Energy is closely related to intention. Intention comes from our invisible inner structure. Intention guides attention by using up energy. Mastering energy requires stalking how one uses up one's energy and therefore where one puts one's attention, which implies reviewing what is using up one's energy and what is attracting one's attention and then making the necessary internal and external adjustments so as to experience a greater control over one's life.

This also requires inner silence so as to « feel » how things are with one's entire being. Inner silence means switching off the always thinking mind that creates continuous internal dialogue, which, from a spiritual point of view, is like a very loud radio permanently making a lot of noise. It also requires becoming free from any self-importance (ego) and from personal history, which includes the various memories (personal, family and past lives). Becoming free means here to recognize what is, to accept it and to integrate it.

There are different courses and exercises to practice inner silence and to become free from personal history and self-importance. Before that, there are readings, books and teachings that help understand reality's and human soul's structures, express in words the path one must take and the goals one much achieve. Books and teachings help build a take-off runway that leads to action and to inner experience. This book shows one of the ways to describe and to perceive the human soul's invisible structure in its central part so as to become more aware of one's identity and of one's evolutionary path. Since a few decades, the Mayan civilization is being revived from its ashes and is resurfacing. Mayan writing is almost fully decrypted and Mayan people in Central America are starting to recover their heritage.

Different Mayan people

From 1200 BC to 400 BC: Olmec Civilization
From 800 BC to 500 BC: Zapotec Civilization
From 300 BC to 750 AD: Teotihuacan Civilization
From 1000 AD to 1150 AD: Toltec Civilization
From 1100 AD to 1550 AD: Aztec Civilization

Mayan Civilization: Part of humanity's heritage

Right from about 400 BC the Mayans built cities and "city-states". Amazing monuments and archeological sites are slowly being restored. The Mayan had books called "codex or codices". Most of them were burned by the Catholics. Only a few survived, amongst which:

- The **Trocortesianus Codex** also called the Madrid Codex
- The **Dresdensis Codex** also called the Dresden Codex
- The **Peresianus Codex** also called the Paris Codex
- The **Grolier Codex** whose authenticity is denied by certain people

Aztec Codices

Borbonicus Codex: ISBN: 3-201-00901-6
Ixtlilxochitl Codex: ISBN: 3-201-00970-9
Magliabechiano Codex: ISBN: 3-201-00763-3
Borgia Codex: ISBN: 3-201-00964-4
Cospi Codex: ISBN: 3-201-00762-5
Fejéváry-Mayer Codex: ISBN: 3-201-00764-1
Laud Codex: ISBN: 3-201-00761-7
Vaticanus 3738 Codex: ISBN: 3-201-01107-X
Vaticanus 3773 Codex: ISBN: 3-201-00780-3

Mixtec Codices

Egerton 2895 Codex Vindobonensis Mexicanus 1 Codex
Zouche-Nuttall Codex Becker I / II Codex

Locating Mayan groups and cities»

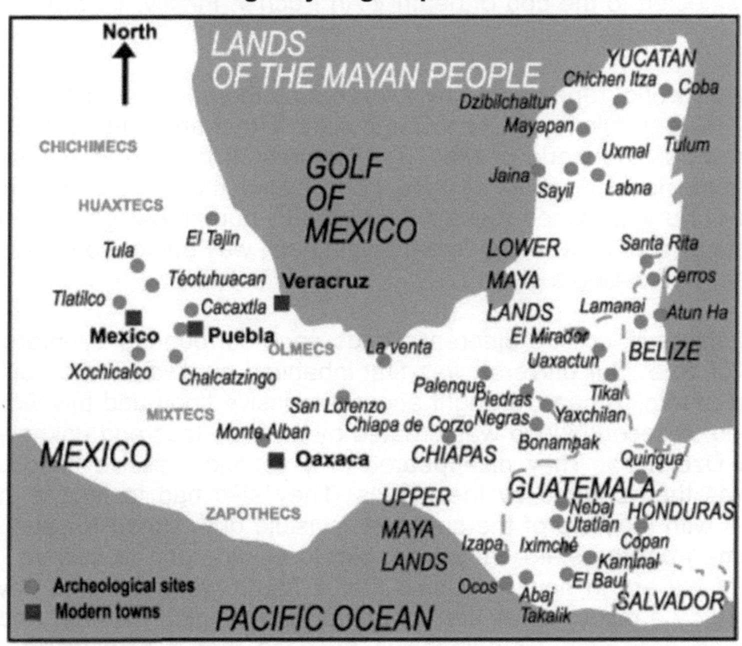

Short description of the Mayan's vision of the world

The Mayan civilization has produced two books, the « Chilam Balam » and the « Popol Vuh ». They were written after the Spanish invasions.
The Mayan pantheon includes numerous gods, natural forces and ancestors. A same god can have a different appearance depending on his age and on wether he is showing his luminous aspect or his dark aspect. These beings organize life according to cycles where creation phases are followed by times of destruction so as to start a new cycle. The world being dark and chaotic, certain Mayan people believed that human sacrifices were necessary to appease the god's anger.

The main Mayan God, who comes from the galactic center, is called "Hunab Ku". He is the creator of everything and because he is invisible, he is not represented. His son, "Itzamma", rules over writing and science. He is the god of the sky and he manifests himself through "Ahau", the sun. His wife, « I x Chel », the moon, rules over child birth, plants, medicine and wellness.

Then there is « Tchaak », the god of rain, represented as a snake. He brings the rain that enables plant growth and harvesting but he can also create downpours and floods. The god of maize is called "Yumtaax". The god of wind is called « Kukulkan ». « Ek Chuah » is the god of war, which is often connected to the god of death « Ah Puch ». Finally, « Xamen ek », is the god who guides Men.

The Mayan world, represented by a three, has three levels. The sky level is ruled by thirteen "sky" gods or « Oxlahuntiku » that are sent by the galactic center towards the world of Men. They represent thirteen intentions. The underground level is ruled by nine gods called the lords of the night or « Bolon Ti Ku ». Between these two levels live human beings were the sun manifests himself in twenty different ways, each way being represented by a pictural symbol called a glyph.

Time is also split up into different worlds each surrounded by intermediate periods of time. Our universe was first inhabited by dwarfs who built cities. The god of rain, Tchaak, brought about a massive flood and this world was destroyed. A second world was created by a mysterious and unknown race called « Dzolobs ». They disappeared in a second massive flood. A third world was then created by the Mayas. They also had to face a massive flood but with the help of the supreme invisible god Hunad Ku and people who came from the stars, they managed to escape and to survive. This is the world we are in now. It is said that a fourth world will one day exist, populated by a mix up of all the human groups mingled together and that it too will be destroyed by a massive flood so that a new world can be created.

Mayan calendars and the counting system

Numbers and glyphs

Mayans loved numbers and their symbolism. They were excellent at observing and were able to handle complex information systems. As time went by, they learned to establish processes, using mathematical constants, which enabled them to predict, with great preciseness, solar and lunar eclipses but also the movement of the visible planets around the sun. Only powerful computer can do that nowadays. Numbers making up natural cycles were represented as sacred pictural symbols or glyphs. Every month, every day, every step of the nine day cycle and of the thirteen day cycle is represented by a glyph. Certain glyphs only represent numbers while others represent objects, animals, people or manifestations of nature.

Agricultural calendar in base 20

The Mayans had several calendars. The two most important numbers used in their calendars are the numbers twenty which was linked to the sun and the number thirteen which was connected with the moon.

They counted in base 20 instead of in base 10 like we do in Europe. The solar civilian agricultural calendar called the Haab calendar was divided into eighteen months (Uinal) of twenty days, to which was added a special period of five days (Uayeb), which gives us 365 days. Each month was represented by a glyph and was linked to a specific event symbolized by a specific god or by a sacred animal. The number twenty is also in connection with the twenty fingers of the human body.

The number thirteen is in connection with the thirteen joints existing in the human body and with the thirteen new annual moons that once took place on planet earth (now there are only twelve except from time to time). There are thirteen intentions or tones that set in motion, as does a wheel, the twenty days which are twenty ways in which the sun expresses itself. The sun symbolizes the god of creation manifesting in the world of matter. These thirteen intentions are like thirteen phases of life on Earth or thirteen series of human experiences.

Every one of the twenty solar manifestations was also represented by a glyph that symbolizes a god, a sacred animal or a sacred object. Every manifestation was celebrated each day. An intention and a solar glyph then combine together to create what is called a "galactic signature" or "Kin". A kin shows the energy of the day, combining solar and moon influence.

The most ancient archeological known traces of these calendars are dated 700 BC.

The sacred calendar based on number thirteen.

The sacred calendar, used to build Mayan charts, is called TzolKin, Tzol meaning to count and Kin meaning day or "the energy of the day". This calendar is made up of thirteen periods of time called tones. Each tonality lasts for twenty days and so this calendar has two hundred and sixty days. The thirteen steps are connected to thirteen goals, intentions or wills coming from the creator of the universe. They are represented by numbers, from one to thirteen. The Mayans described then as cosmic energies emerging from the galactic center.

The twenty solar day and the thirteen intentions or tones can be combined together to create 52 year cycles. The number 52 was very important for the Mayans.

Other calendars

A first counting system combines the civilian agricultural calendar with the sacred calendar to create an 18980 (365*52) days or 52 year cycle. A second counting system, called the long count calendar, adds up different time lengths, just like we add up units, dozens, hundreds and thousands; except that here, we are counting in base twenty. A third counting system also exists in base thirteen.

Long count calendar

UNITS	NAME OF THE PERIOD	LINK WITH THE PREVIOUS UNIT	CALCULATION	NUMBER OF DAYS	NUMBER OF YEARS
1	KIN =DAY	0		1	0
2	UINAL=Month of 20 days	20 kin	1X20	20	0
3	TUN=Year of 18 months	18 uinal	18X20	360	1
4	KATUN=Cycle of 20 "years"	20 tun	20X360	7 200	20
5	BAKTUN=Cycle of 400 "years"	20 katun	20X7200	144 000	400
6	PICTUN=Cycle of 8 000"years"	20 baktun	20X144 000	2 880 000	8000
7	CALABTUN=Cycle of 160 000 "years"	20 pictun	20X2 880 000	57 600 000	160 000
8	KINCHILTUN=Cycle of 3 200 000 "years"	20 calabtun	20 x 57 600 000	1 152 000 000	3 200 000
9	ALAUTUN=Cycle of 640 000 000 "years"	20 kinchiltun	20 x 1 152 000 000 000	23 040 000 000	640 000 000

The days of the sacred Maya calendar

THE TONES			THE GLYPHS	Yukatek Maya name	Quiché Maya Name	Archeological translation	Thirteen moon Calendar name	Thirteen moon Calendar name Glyph
•	1	The Original intention The impulse that triggers		IMIX	IMOX	Life tree crocodile Milky way	DRAGON	
••	2	The Duality that stimulates		IK	IQ	Breath The wind	WIND	
•••	3	Movement that sets life in action		AKBAL	AQABAL	To give House	NIGHT	
••••	4	Foundations that anchor and stabilize		KAN	KAT	Maize seed Lizard Jewel	SEED	
—	5	Expression of power that enables self-realization		CHICCHAN	KAN	Celestial Snake	SNAKE	
— •	6	The flow of intelligence that enables adaptation		CIMI	KAME	Black Death	DEATH OR BRIDGE	
— ••	7	Strategic action that reveals what is important		MANIK	KEJ	To take Hand Deer	HAND	
— •••	8	Justice that creates balance and harmony		LAMAT	QUANIL	Star Venus Rabbit	STAR	
— ••••	9	Expansion that creates motion		MULUC	TOJ	Payment Water	MOON	
═	10	Building one's accomplishment		OC	TZI	Foot Dog	DOG	

	Number	Meaning	Glyph	Maya	Alt	Description	English
•̣ (bar symbol)	11	Clarification that enables improvements		CHU EN	BATZ	Craftsman Monkey	MONKEY
•• (bar symbol)	12	Assimilation and understanding that allow renewal		EB	EE	Messenger Herb Road	HUMAN
••• (bar symbol)	13	Going beyond one's self to co-create with the universe		BEN	AJ	Reed Maize	SKY WALKER
				IX	HIX	Woman Jaguar Wisdom	MAGICIAN
	Zero			MEN	TZIKIN	Bird Master Eagle	EAGLE
0		Origin and destination		CIB	AJMAAQ	Honey Vulture Owl	WARRIOR
(glyph)				CAB AN	NOJ	Earth Movement	EARTH
				ETZ NAB	TIJAZ	Flint Mirror	MIROR
				CAU AC	KAWOQ	Storm Rain	STORM
				AHA U	AJPU	Flower Sun Lord	SUN

Why is number thirteen so important?

For the Mayas, number thirteen symbolizes motion, cycles and the end of something. The body has thirteen joints that enable movement. In previous eras, a full moon occurred thirteen times per year until, according to a Mayan legend, an astronomical event that created disasters on Earth around 3500 BC put an end to this. Since that event, years where there are thirteen moons are very rare and special.

If you consider the length of time called Pictun (400 years) and if you count in base thirteen instead of base twenty, then thirteen times four hundred years gives you five thousand and two hundred years. In 2012, the thirteenth Baktun came to an end. At the same time, an astronomical event, that only occurs twice every 26800 years, called the galactic cross, occurred between 1986 and 2012 (see annex). Because the number thirteen has a very strong symbolic meaning, the Mayans said that these times pinpoint the end of a world and the beginning of a new era, and certainly not the end of "The World". The concept of "the end of the world" is created by the "always thinking mind" and does not exist in Reality. According to the Mayas, the world has no end. It breathes like a living being in extremely long expansion and contraction cycles.

The four colors of Mayan glyphs.

The twenty Mayan glyphs are organized in four families of four different colors. These colors are connected to the four directions and to the four great families that originally populated planet Earth.

The Reds are the ones who trigger events, the undertakers, and the creative people. They are said to rule over east according to the agricultural calendar. **(Red glyphs: the Dragon, the Snake, Water or the Moon, the Skywalker and the Earth)**

The Whites are those who structure, organize and realize. They are builders. They are said to rule over north according to the agricultural calendar. **(White glyphs : The Wind or Spirit, Death or the Bridge, the Dog, the Jaguar or Magician and the Mirror or Flintstone)**

The blues or browns are those who enable conscious and intensive presence within the body, vision and awareness, putting things into form, making adjustments, bringing about changes and working with groups. They are said to rule over West. **(Blue glyphs: the Night, the Hand, the Monkey, the Eagle and the Rain or Storm)**

The yellows are artists that have creative power, organization capabilities and transformation abilities. They create expansion and maturity. They bring things to the best of what they can be thanks to the mastery of networks, information systems and emotion. They are said to rule over the south according to the agricultural calendar. **(Yellow glyphs: the Seed, the Star, the Human, the warrior or Vulture and the Sun).** At the center of these four colors lives the green color. It symbolizes the center, awareness, the heart and the necessary pathway to bring about the great transformation process that brings one back to a reconnection with the galactic center.

The twenty glyphs have also each a direction, in the same east, north, west and south sequence. Reds and Blues are complementary opposites that challenge and surprise one another. Same with Yellows and Whites.

The Reds and the Whites naturally get on very well, just as Yellow and Blues. A person born under a white identity glyph, for example, will also naturally get on well with people who are also born under white identity glyphs. Other relationships are more challenging. Finally, glyphs that rule over similar directions, whatever their colors usually get on well even if they are very different.

Modern Mayan calendars currently used.

Spanish religious authorities having destroyed almost all Mayan books between 1492 and 1800 AD, most of the Mayan knowledge was lost. Centuries of research have tried to recover this knowledge. This book therefore deals with Mayan astrology according to what is currently known.
When Spanish missionaries discovered Mayan culture, they tried to match Mayan calendars with their own, which at the time was the Christian Julian calendar. The most famous of these missionaries, Diego de Landa (1524-1579) wrote « Relationships of Yucatan things», after burning all the books he could get his hands on.

A number called « correlation constant » enables the conversion of a Maya date into a Christian Gregorian date. With all the technology and resources we currently have, there isn't yet an international agreement defining with certainty the correct correlation constant. And yet, practice gives amazing results.

Two main calendars have emerged from archeological, historical and personal research undertaken these past decades and centuries. Each of the two calendars focuses on a different vision and describes reality at different levels, a bit like the Sun and the Moon enlighten two parts of reality or show a same reality in two different ways. The two calendars described in this book therefore show two complementary visions.

The thirteen moon calendar:

The first calendar rediscovered, so to say, was called the thirteen moon calendar. It was created by Mister and Missus Argüelles in the 1970's. This calendar which is a simplified version of the Mayan calendar, has greatly contributed to make people know about Mayan astrology and culture. In this calendar, the day starts at 00.00 am and ends at 24.00 pm.

It was created using the Yukatek Mayan agricultural calendar and other esoterical elements. It describes a path enabling a person to adapt to the world of matter. It uses a modified GMT correlation constant (584283).

The calendar called the traditional calendar:

This second calendar was spread more recently in the west by a Swedish scientist called Johann Calleman. The beginning of the day starts here at sunrise which implies knowing exactly when sunrise takes place. I use astrological software to do this. The time of sunrise is when the ascendant reaches the Sun's position. This calendar is connected to the vision of Quitché and Tcholan Mayas and to the sacred calendar which deals with the evolution of consciousness. It uses what is called the GMT correlation constant (584283). This constant is recognized as correct by many Mayan communities. Certain researchers and scientists do not agree with it.

The two calendars place five glyphs in a cross like pattern that reveals a person's structure and then thirteen glyphs in a sequence which reveals an evolutionary path. The names of the glyphs are different depending on the calendar used.

Just for information, a Belgian scientist and researcher, Doctor Antoon Leon Vollemaere, suggest that the correct correlation constant (VMR) should be 774079 for people born before midday and 774080 for people born after midday. I have done some research using this constant and my first conclusion is that it does reveal part of the soul's reality, but the first two calendars seem to be much more relevant. The Bohn brothers, also scientists, suggest using 662261 as the correct correlation constant.

Only appropriate research in linguistics, astronomy, archeology, history and astrology will one day give clear explanations and confirm with certainty which constant is the right one, if there is a "right one".

Structure of a Mayan Chart

The five glyphs of the Mayan cross: A Mayan chart is first made up of an oracle, i.e. a series of five glyphs out of a possible total of twenty. Each glyph is linked to one of the thirteen tones. The tonality gives the glyph a specific color.

The glyphs are like genetic activation codes, galactic information codes, ideal vibratory models, archetypes, behavioral models and autonomous wills that are activated and brought to life by the thirteen tones. If we dare make a comparison with western astrology, the twenty solar glyphs can be considered as astrological signs or as planets while the thirteen tones can be considered as astrological houses or sectors. We then have a combination sign-house or planet-house.

The Mayans considered the glyphs as gods. These five glyphs are spread out in the shape of a cross. This cross is called the Mayan Cross. The glyphs represent the masculine part of a human being.

The thirteen steps of the evolutionary path: A Mayan chart is secondly made up of an evolutionary path that has thirteen steps or experience fields.

This path is connected to the central identity glyph. This evolutionary path is called the "Enchanted path" in the "Thirteen moon calendar" and the "Trecena" or a "Wavespell" in the "Traditional Mayan calendar".

 It describes a vibratory frequency or state of being that determines what your life task is and the abilities that are necessary to accomplish this mission. It describes a pathway towards yourself to serve life or the universe and to accomplish who you are in a very practical manner, though life and action, in thirteen steps.

This thirteen step pathway is also a manner to describe any evolutionary process or project. A Mayan chart finally has what is called « the lord of the night » and also numerological cycles. These represent the feminine part of a human being.

Example of a Mayan Cross

THE "ORIGIN" GLYPH OR "BIRTHGUIDE" GLYPH

THE EARTH

THE ANTIPODE OR CHALLENGE GLYPH

THE BIRTH GLYPH OR KIN

THE ANALOGUE OR ALLY GLYPH

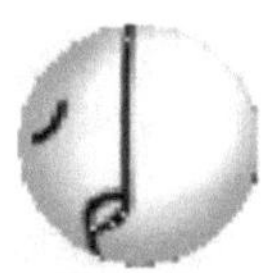

THE NIGHT

THE SKYWALKER

DEATH OR THE BRIDGE OR THE WORLD BRIDGER

THE OCCULT OR DESTINATION GLYPH

THE STAR

The Mayan Cross with traditional glyphs

CONCEPTION KIN

MANIK-HAND-7

MASCULINE KIN CHALLENGE

MULUK MOON-9

BIRTH KIN

MEN EAGLE-2

FEMININE KIN SUPPORT

IMIX-DRAGON-6

DESTINATION KIN

AKBAL-NIGHT-10

Your birth glyph or identity glyph

The identity glyph is the one at the center of the cross. It describes your landmarks, your life ideal and the main guidelines of your destiny. It is with the help of this glyph that you can center yourself, find your personal galactic center and reconnect yourself with the galactic source and its flow of light and love. This is your wall socket where you have to plug in the electrical outlet so that electrical current flows within you and lights up the thin metal wire at the center of the light bulb

The origin or conception glyph

This glyph is just above the identity glyph. It describes a resource you are born with and how you can acquire wisdom using this resource. It is the energy showing where you come from, your conception energy that influences how you learn and how you evolve in this lifetime. It may be a little excessive during the first part of life. The more you express this glyph in a balanced manner, in full awareness and the more you will learn and evolve.

The analogue or ally glyph

This glyph is located at the right hand side of the identity glyph. It shows an energy that naturally helps you and supports you whatever the situation or the relationship that occurs. It is your ally so when you are with it, things progress. It is a natural resource you can call upon but it only manifests itself if you call upon it, which you tend to do instinctively, without always being aware of it.

The antipode or challenge glyph

This glyph is located at the left hand side of the identity glyph. It describes the energy that is the most different or opposite of how you see yourself or the energy that you are the most, at first, unaware of. It is like a part of you that has been lost and that you must recover and allow to become part of you again. This energy is therefore a challenge for you. It is there to make you question yourself, to make you move and to make you progress. It may be connected to obstacles, fears, difficult situations or people that are totally opposite and different from you. This glyph is however your greatest teacher or master as it can enable you to surpass yourself and to greatly evolve.
 Its energy is the one that can most help you see who you really are and the one that can most help you become aware.

The destination or occult glyph

This glyph is located just below the identity glyph. It represents a great potential that can however only be revealed and developed through work on yourself and if your surpass yourself. It can be extremely helpful especially when your usual resources fail to solve an issue and bring results. You can call upon this glyph when all your conscious resources have been unsuccessfully used. If the skills and abilities symbolized by this glyph are not recognized and developed consciously, they remain asleep in the unconscious self. This glyph represents where you must go in life, the direction you must take to evolve, the qualifications you must develop and the program you must achieve.

The two numbers connected to each glyph: Each glyph goes along with two numbers. The first number is its position in the sequence of twenty glyphs, between one for the first glyph (the dragon) and twenty for the last glyph (the sun). The second important number is the value of the glyph when it is combined with one of the thirteen tones. As there are 260 possible combinations, a glyph can be numbered between one and two hundred and sixty.

Example: A dragon glyph of tonality nine (one bar and four dots) has a value of 61 as shown in table 3 at the end of the book. The dragon's position is 1.

Annual forecasts:

In the thirteen moon calendar, the identity glyph corresponding to the date of July 26th colors, at a global collective level, the Mayan year which, according to this calendar, starts on July 26. It is then a good year to express what the identity glyph symbolizes.

At an individual level, you can calculate and interpret the Mayan cross on your annual birthday. The identity glyph then shows what will be important during the year and what can help you become more aware of your identity. The ally glyph shows what helps you during the year while the antipode or challenge glyph shows you where efforts will have to be made. The origin glyph shows you what can guide you during while the destination glyph shows you what must be understood and integrated. The first glyph of the evolutionary path shows you what talents will have to be used during the year or a project to work on. This analysis can give you a very interesting look and some landmarks. It's up to you to experiment. You can observe that with the thirteen moon calendar, the same five glyphs follow one another in a cyclic pattern.

<u>Calculating and drawing the Mayan Cross</u>
<u>According to the thirteen moon calendar</u>

A series of tables will easily allow you to calculate and find the five glyphs of your Mayan Cross according to the thirteen moon calendar.

The day starts at midday in this calendar.

How to calculate the identity glyph

Look at **table 1** to find and note the conversion constant corresponding to the year of birth. (See page 161)

Look at **table 2** to find and note the conversion constant corresponding to the day and month of birth. (See page 163)

Add the two numbers previously found. This is the number of your identity kin. In **table 3,** locate the total you have just calculated. Above the number, the bars and dots give you the totality of your identity glyph. Move left along the page to locate you identity glyph.

Example for a person born on the fifth of January 2000:

Table 1 indicates 98 as the year constant for year 2000.
Table 2 indicates 59 as the day and month constant for January the 5th.

98 + 59 = 157

When you look at table 3 and find number 157, you can see one black circle • above number 157. The tonality for this glyph is one. When you go to the left of the page, you can see that the corresponding glyph is Earth. The identity glyph is therefore earth with a tonality of one. In the thirteen moon calendar, tonality number one is called magnetic. The identity glyph is therefore Magnetic Earth.

If the number found when adding the numbers in tables 1 and 2 is greater than 260, then subtract 260 from the total you have found.

You have a calculator on the website 13lunas.net.

Tables can be found in the appendix at the end of the book.

The four remaining glyphs are calculated using the identity glyph

How to calculate the origin or guiding glyph

The twenty glyphs follow one another according to a specific sequence, starting with the Dragon who is glyph number 1. The origin glyph always has a value corresponding to a number between one and twenty. This value corresponds to the position of the glyph we are looking for within the twenty glyph sequence.

In our example, we had found 157 as the value of the identity glyph

See **Table 4** page 170. The origin glyph is showed by the number above number 157, which in this case is number 17. The origin glyph is therefore the seventeenth glyph in the sequence of twenty, i.e. Earth glyph.

The origin glyph is quite often the same as the identity glyph.

How to calculate the ally glyph

The ally glyph always has a value corresponding to a number between one and twenty.

The total of the identity glyph's position and the ally glyph's position must be equal to 19. 19 – Identity glyph's position = Ally glyph's position.

In our example, the value corresponding to the identity glyph's position is 17. Earth glyph is the seventeenth glyph in the sequence of twenty. So 19-17=2. The ally glyph is here therefore the glyph which is in position number two in the twenty glyph sequence, which is the wind glyph.

Special cases: If the position if your identity glyph is 20, the sun, then the ally glyph will be 20-1=19 which gives us the storm glyph. If the position if your identity glyph is 19, the storm, then the ally glyph will be 19-19=0 which gives us the sun glyph. The sun glyph has a value of twenty or zero.

How to calculate the antipode glyph

The antipode glyph always has a different color than the identity glyph.

It is found by adding or subtracting ten to the value of the identity kin. Antipode glyph = identity kin plus or minus 10. You will find the same glyph wether you add or subtract 10. (See table 3 on page 168).

In our example, the value of the identity kin (glyph with its tonality) or glyph is 157. The antipode glyph is therefore 157 +-10 which equals either 167 or 147. For both of these values, the corresponding glyph is the Hand (Manik).

How to calculate the occult glyph

The occult glyph always has a value corresponding to a number between one and twenty. **The total of the identity glyph's position and the occult glyph's position must be equal to 21. 21 – Identity glyph's position = Occult glyph's position.**

In our example, the origin glyph is in position 17. 17+4=21. 21-17=4. The occult glyph is the one in position four which is the seed.

We therefore have : Earth with tonality one or « Magnetic Earth » as identity kin and glyph, the Earth also as origin or guiding glyph, the Wind as Ally glyph, the Hand as antipode glyph and the Seed as occult or destination glyph.

This can be shown as follows

**THE "ORIGIN"
GLYPH OR
"BIRTHGUIDE"
GLYPH**

THE EARTH

THE ANTIPODE OR CHALLENGE GLYPH	**THE IDENTITY OR BIRTH GLYPH OR KIN**	**THE ANALOGUE OR ALLY GLYPH**

THE HAND	**THE EARTH-1**	**THE WIND**

**THE OCCULT OR
DESTINATION
GLYPH**

THE SEED

How to calculate the evolutionary path also called the enchanted path or the dream spell.

If you observe table 3 and start at the very first kin, the dragon of tonality one, you will see that the glyphs are organized in sequences of thirteen. The fourteenth glyph therefore starts the second series of thirteen glyphs. These sequences or series of thirteen glyphs make up the evolutionary path in thirteen steps.

The evolutionary path is calculated by using the identity glyph's tonality. The beginning of the evolutionary path can be found by finding the tonality of the identity glyph and then by going backwards until tonality one of this specific sequence is reached.

If, as in our example of a person born on the 2nd of January 2000 who has an identity glyph of tonality one, then the beginning of the evolutionally path is the same as the identity glyph. Step one of the evolutionary path is therefore Earth with tonality 1.

If the value of the Identity glyph had been 158,159,160,161,162,163,164,165,166,167,168 or 169, we would also have gone backwards towards the glyph with tonality one, in his case the Earth glyph.

You then note, in this case starting with glyph 157 (tonality 1), the thirteen steps or houses of the evolutionary path, that is:

STEP 1: Earth
STEP 2: Mirror
STEP 3: Storm
STEP 4: Sun
STEP 5: Dragon
STEP 6: Wind
STEP 7: Night
STEP 8: Seed
STEP 9: Snake
STEP 10: Bridge
STEP 11: Hand
STEP 12: Star
STEP 13: Moon

This can be represented graphically as in the following scheme.

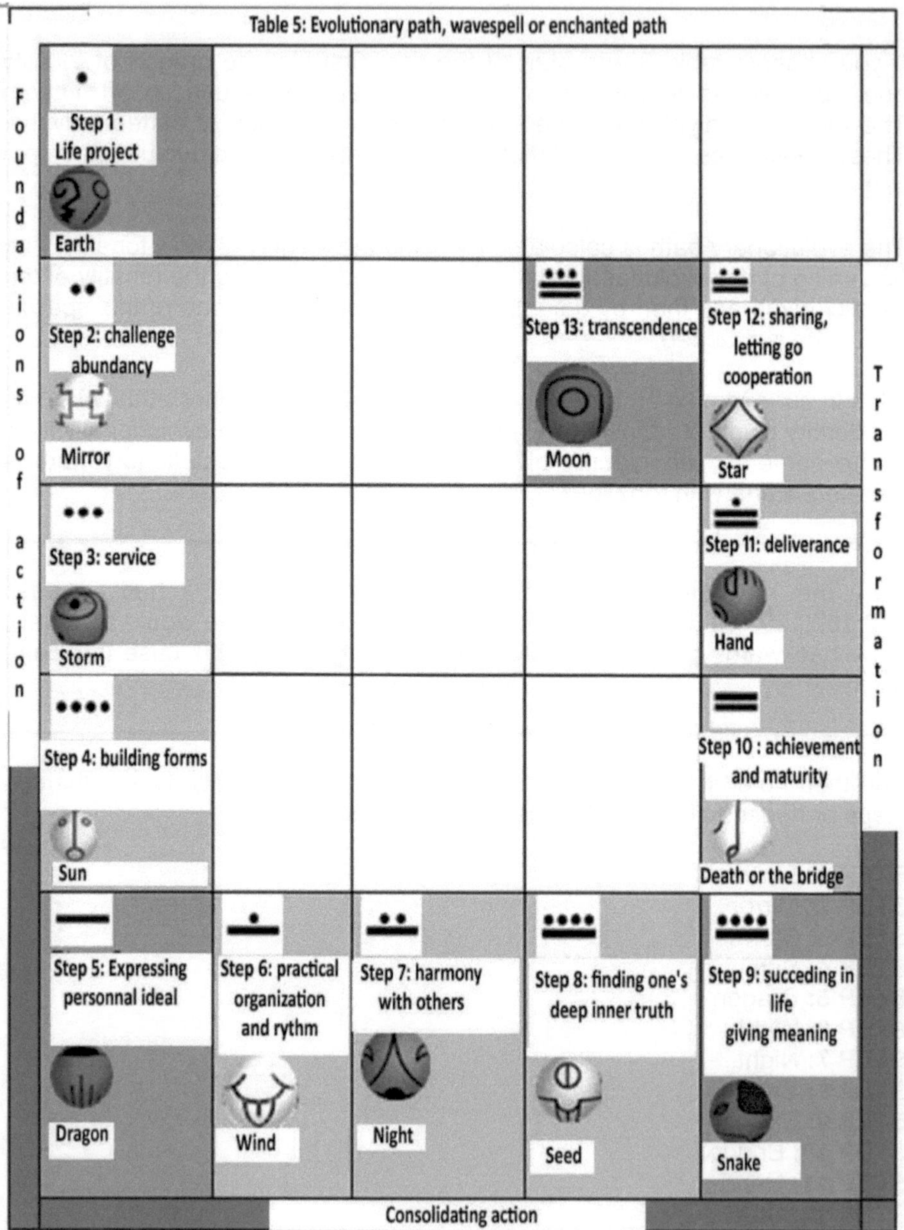

You can notice that:

Houses 1, 5, 9 and 13, in grey, are the angular stones of the path. They represent the eternal spiritual body and its evolution in four steps, the encounter, integration, deliverance and transcendence.

Houses 2, 6 and 10 are like a step 1. They represent the physical body, life embodied, expression of the senses in matter and its evolution in three steps, encountering matter, integrating matter and deliverance from matter which leads to fullness.

Houses 3, 7 and 11 are like a step 2. They represent the soul body, emotions and social intelligence expressing itself within the environment in three steps, encountering others, integrating relationships and emotional deliverance leading to fullness.

Houses 4, 8 and 12 are like a step 3. They represent the psychic body and soul power in three steps, encountering form and construction, integrating form and adapting to all frequencies of reality and deliverance from form through cooperation, which also leads to fullness.

Those of you who are familiar with western astrology will see that the first group matches the fire element, the second group the earth element, the third group the air element and the fourth group the water element. You can also notice that the first twelve houses match very closely western and eastern astrological houses. Mayans call the path the Wavespell or enchanted path because they consider it to be like a wave that is capable of bringing the soul towards enlightment.

<u>Calculating and drawing the Mayan Cross</u>
<u>According to the traditional calendar</u>

In this calendar, the day starts when the sun rises above the horizon just as the year starts at the spring equinox around March 21rst.

How to calculate the identity glyph

You need your day, month, year and hour of birth.

Note your year of birth

Rule: If you are born between January the first and march the twentieth included, take away one year from your birth year.

STEP 1: Find and note the birth year conversion constant using table 5. (Page 173)

STEP 2: Find and note the birth day and month conversion constant using table 6. (Page 175).

Rule: If you are born between midnight and sunrise, take away one day from your birth day and month of birth.

STEP 3: Add the two values and seek the corresponding number in table 3.

Rule: If the number found when adding the numbers in tables 6 and 7 is greater than 260, then subtract 260 from the total you have found.

Example of a person born on the second of January 2001 at two a.m.

Table 5 gives a value of 52 for year 2000. (Take the previous year because the person is born before March 21rst).

Table 6 gives a value of 26 for the first of January. (You take the previous day for people born before sunrise).

52 + 26 = **78** so the identity kin is **78.**

STEP 4: When you check the glyph corresponding to number 78 in table 7 page 177, you can see that the corresponding glyph is the rabbit glyph. You identify the Identity glyph as been the Rabbit or the Star. The picture with bars and dots shows the tonality which here is thirteen.

You can also use the calculator on the websitemaya-portal.net and go to the website http://www.pauahtun.org/cgi-bin/gregmaya.py to check the lord of the night by imputing 584283 as the conversion constant.

How to calculate the origin glyph

The value of the Origin glyph can be found by subtracting eight to the value of the Identity glyph. In our example, the Identity glyph is 78 so 78-8=**70**. If you check table 7 page 176, you will see that this corresponds to the Sun glyph with a tonality of five.

The Origin glyph's color is the same as the color of the Identity Glyph.

How to calculate the Ally glyph

The value of the Ally glyph can be found by adding six to the value of the Identity glyph. In our example, the Identity glyph is 78 so 78+6=**84**. If you check table 7 page 176, you will see that this corresponds to the Jaguar or Magician glyph with a tonality of six.

How to calculate the antipode glyph

The value of the Antipode glyph can be found by subtracting six to the value of the Identity glyph.

In our example, the Identity glyph is 78 so 78-6=**72**. If you check table 7 page 176, you will see that this corresponds to the Wind glyph with a tonality of seven.

How to calculate the occult glyph

The value of the Antipode glyph can be found by adding eight to the value of the Identity glyph. In our example, the Identity glyph is 78 so 78+8=**86**. If you check table 7 page 176, you will see that this corresponds to the Warrior or Vulture glyph with a tonality of eight.

We therefore have: The rabbit glyph with tonality 13 as Identity glyph, the Sun with tonality 5 as Origin glyph, the Jaguar or Magician with tonality 6 as Ally glyph, the Wine with tonality 7 as Antipode glyph or Challenge glyph and the Warrior with tonality 8 as Destination glyph.

THE ORIGIN GLYPH

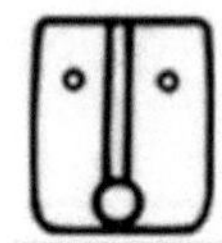

Ahau-Sun-5

THE CHALLENGE GLYPH

THE IDENTITY GLYPH

THE ALLY GLYPH

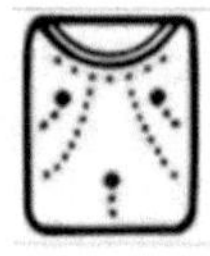

Kin 78

Ix - Magician-6

Ik-Wind-7

Lamat- Star - 13

THE DESTINATION GLYPH

Cib - Warrior – 8

How to calculate the evolutionary path or Trecena

If you observe table 8 and start at the very first kin, the Monkey of tonality one, you will see that the glyphs are organized in sequences of thirteen. The fourteenth glyph therefore starts a second series of thirteen glyphs. These sequences or series of thirteen glyphs make up the evolutionary path which is called the "Trecena" in the traditional calendar.

The evolutionary path is calculated by using the tonality of the Identity glyph. The beginning of the evolutionary path can be found by finding the tonality of the identity glyph and then by going backwards until tonality one of this specific sequence is reached. A Trecena always begins with a tonality of one and ends with a tonality of thirteen.

If, the tonality of the Identity glyph is one, then the beginning of the evolutionally path is the same as the identity glyph. If the tonality of the Identity glyph is thirteen as it is the case here, then you must go back towards the tonality one of the same sequence. Doing so brings us to the Warrior or Vulture glyph of tonality one. Step one of the evolutionary path is therefore Warrior with tonality 1.

STEP 1: The Warrior. Life project or initial intention is here connected to the Warrior.

STEP 2: The Earth. The challenge of dual energy that leads to action. How to create abundance in matter is here connected to the Earth.

STEP 3: The Flintstone or Mirror. Movement leading to service is here connected to the Flintstone or Mirror.

STEP 4: The Storm. Stabilizing foundations by organizing matter.

STEP 5: The Sun. Expressing personal power.

STEP 6: The Dragon or Alligator. Practical adaptation using intelligence and organization of data.

STEP 7: The Wind. Being balanced and connecting to civilization.

STEP 8: The Night or House. Seeking one's deep inner truth and being in harmony with eternal laws.

STEP 9: The Lizard or Seed. Finding one's place in the world, developing one's abilities through action and living one's life.

STEP 10: The Snake. Building one's destiny and achieving self-realization.

STEP 11: Death or the Bridge. Bringing about clarity, improvement, solutions and inner freedom.

STEP 12: The Deer or the Hand. Assimilating, experiencing communion and cooperating in collective activities.

STEP 13: The Rabbit or the Star. Experiencing transcendence and helping the universe to make humanity progress. This is here connected to the Rabbit or the Star.

It is important to notice what glyphs of the Trecena sequence are in the Mayan cross and where they are. The Trecena can be represented graphically as follows:

OWL OR VULTURE OR WARRIOR TRECENA

You are now ready to interpret.

Interpretation of a Mayan chart

The Mayan cross

STEP 1: You interpret the Identity glyph.

It's important to talk about the glyph's color and about the positive relationship with glyphs of the same color.

STEP 2: You interpret the tonality that is linked with the glyph. This is a number between one and thirteen. You can synthesize the Identity glyph and its tonality

STEP 3: You interpret the guide or Origin glyph.

STEP 4: You interpret the Ally glyph on the right hand side of the Mayan cross.

STEP 5: You interpret the Antipode or Challenge glyph on the left hand side of the Mayan cross.

You can compare the two Ally and Antipode glyphs and synthesize.

STEP 6: You interpret the Occult or de Destination glyph at the bottom of the Mayan cross.

You can compare the two Origin-Destination glyphs and synthesize.

The evolutionary path

It is also called wave, enchanted wave or Dreamspell in the thirteen moon calendar and the « Trecena » in the traditional calendar.

STEP 0: Take a look at the houses in the evolutionary path that occupied by glyphs that are also part of the Mayan Cross. These houses are important experience fields.

STEP 1: Interpret the glyph in house 1 and describe the life project. Compare the « Life project » with the Identity glyph.

STEP 2: Interpret the glyph in house 2 and describe the main challenge. Compare this with the antipode glyph. Describe how the person can create his material and spiritual abundance.

STEP 3: Interpret the glyph in house 3 and describe how the person can communicate, adapt and serve. Compare this with the Ally glyph which can be a great help to serve.

STEP 4: Interpret the glyph in house 4 and describe how the person organizes his daily life, how he puts things into shape and how he builds his foundations and his home. Compare the person's foundations and the Origin glyph.

STEP 5: Interpret the glyph in house 5 and describe how the person expresses his ideals, his creative power, his will and his awareness. Compare his life ideal and his Identity glyph.

STEP 6: Interpret the glyph in house 6 and describe how the person gets organized, how he handles data so as to adapt technically, how he deals with his health and what he experiences in a repetitive manner.

STEP 7: Interpret the glyph in house 7 and describe how the person builds relationships with others and how he creates balance and harmony. Describe what attracts him in others and his main challenge due to the fact that the glyph in house 7 is not naturally integrated. Compare this glyph with the antipode glyph.

STEP 8: Interpret the glyph in house 8 and describe how the person can bring about change in his life and his relationship with life hereafter.

STEP 9: Interpret the glyph in house 9 and describe how the person can express his authority in the world, find his place and play his role as a spiritual being.

STEP 10: Interpret the glyph in house 10 and describe the person's life path, how he builds his goals and how he expresses his ability to be responsible.

STEP 11: Interpret the glyph in house 11 and describe how the person can bring about clarity, improvements and more freedom in his life and in the lives of others.

STEP 12: Interpret the glyph in house 12 and describe how the person can go beyond his limits, how he can cooperate with others within collective undertakings and how he can contribute to heal people's sufferings.

STEP 13: Interpret the glyph in house 13 and describe how the person can experience transcendence and how he can put aside and transform his personal, ancestral and/or past lives memories so as to live his true life.

STEP 14: Compare the glyphs in Houses 1, 5, 9 and 13 to see how the person expresses his energy and awareness.

STEP 15: Compare the glyphs in Houses 2, 6 and 10 to see how the person gets organized within matter.

STEP 16: Compare the glyphs in Houses 3, 7 and 9 to see how the person communicates, expresses his social intelligence and adapts in the external world and within himself.

STEP 17: Compare the glyphs in Houses 4, 8 and 12 to see how the person changes and evolves spiritually.

The lord of the night: (This is specific to the traditional calendar). Here is described the shadow that must be dealt with in order to gain access to inner light.

Mayan Numerology

The Mayans believe two numbers mainly influence cycles, number 13 and number 52. Adding these two numbers creates a third cycle and focuses on special days that have strong vibration, where the soul can eliminate its tensions, purify itself and express itself both at an individual level and at a collective level. These special days were often chosen to undertake rituals or for group games. From a collective point of view, these special days sometimes coincide with times of crisis or strong social tension. At an individual level, these days can coincide with important events, with moments of intense awareness or with times when tensions go away.

13 year cycles

The human soul gains maturity according to 13 year cycles. The first sequence of 13 years represents childhood, the second sequence the learning phase, the third sequence the inner journey, the fourth sequence expressing the master within you and the fifth sequence teaching to others. One of the glyph from the evolutionary path sequence are highlighted every year, along with the house where the glyph is within the 13 glyph sequence. When interpreting, one can highlight the glyph, the step and the number of the 13 year sequence that one can focus on during the year.

Here are the first five 13 year cycles.

Step	Symbol	Main concerns during the year	Ages Phase 1	Ages Phase 2	Ages Phase 3	Ages Phase 4	Ages Phase 5
1		Life project or initial intention	0	13	26	39	52
2		Duality, a chalenge or creating abundance	1	14	27	40	53
3		Movement, learning adapting and serving	2	15	28	41	54
4		Building and stabilizing foundations	3	16	29	42	55
5		Expressing love and personnal power	4	17	30	43	56
6		Practical adaptation through organization	5	18	31	44	57
7		Balance and relationships within civilization	6	19	32	45	58
8		Integration of eternal laws	7	20	33	46	59
9		Finding one's place and expressing oneself in the world	8	21	34	47	60
10		Building one's destiny and undertaking achievements	9	22	35	48	61
11		Clarify and improve to create freedom	10	23	36	49	62
12		Assimilation, communion and cooperation	11	24	37	50	63
13		Transcend and help the universe make humanity progress	12	25	38	51	64

Cycles of 65 day and the burner days

The sacred calendar's 260 day cycle has four special days called burner days. The agricultural calendar starts with the dragon glyph of tonality 1. The first burner day is calculated by adding 65 to the previously mentioned glyph. The second burner day is calculated by again adding 65 and so on until the fourth day. When doing this, you will find that the four burner days are occupied by a monkey glyph of tonality 4, a Sun glyph of tonality 4, an eagle glyph of tonality 4 and a dog glyph of tonality 4. This calculation can also be done with the traditional calendar where you then start counting from the Monkey glyph of tonality 1.

At an individual level, the first burner day is the day occupied by the first glyph of your evolutionary path. The three other burner days can be calculated by adding 65 each time. The first glyph of your evolutionary path and the three other burner days make up a family. People who have one of these glyphs as Identity glyph can have a very strong impact on your evolution. You can build very special relationships with these people. Burner days as special because during these days, you can let go of any excessive energy, emotions, tension and stress.

The following website can help you check this out : http://www.xzone.com.au/maya/main.php

Synthesis

You can then synthesize and conclude. Actions to improve things can be suggested.

Example:

Mister James Redfield was born on 19th march 1950 at 5.30 pm. Just like Carlos Castaneda, Henri Gougaud, Luis Hansa, Don Miguel Ruiz and Victor Sanchez, James Redfield greatly helped to spread Latin American Chamanic culture through his books "The Andes prophecy" and "The tenth prophecy".

A Mayan chart is above all an inner experience and not an analytical process. The example that follows just shows you how to put down the structure of a Mayan Chart and how to compare the 13 moon calendar, the traditional calendar with the GMT (584283) constant and with the VMR (774080) constant. I believe that there are no "right" or "wrong" charts and that it's up to the person concerned to feel what speaks and vibrates most for her or him.

13 Moon calendar

Identity glyph:

Table 1: Constant for the year 1950 =48

Table 2: Constant for the 19th of March = 132. Total=180.

Table 3: Kin 180 is the « Sun glyph» of tonality 11.

The Identity glyph is therefore the Sun with a tonality of eleven.

Table 4: When you observe glyph number 180 on Table 4, the number above 180 gives you the Origin glyph or Guide glyph. Here, number 20 means that the Guide glyph if the twentieth glyph in the sequence of twenty, which is the Sun again.

Ally glyph: 19 – Identity glyph = Ally glyph.

19-20=-1.

When you obtain zero or a negative number, you add twenty to the number you obtain.

-1+20=19, this corresponds to the Storm glyph.

Antipode glyph: Identity glyph + or – 10 gives you glyph number 170 or 190, which corresponds to the Dog glyph.

Occult glyph: Identity glyph + Occult glyph = 21. 20 + Occult glyph = 21. Occult glyph = 21-20=1 which corresponds to the Dragon glyph.

Evolutionary path, enchanted path or Dreamspell: When you go back from tonality 11 to tonality 1, you arrive at glyph number 170, the Dog glyph. You therefore obtain the evolutionary path of the Dog. This means the Dog glyph is in house 1, the Monkey glyph is in house 2, the Human glyph is in house 3, the Skywalker glyph is in house 4, the Jaguar glyph is in house 5, the Eagle glyph is in house 6, the Warrior glyph is in house 7, the Earth glyph is in house 8, the Flint or Mirror glyph is in house 9, the Storm glyph is in house 10, the Sun glyph is in house 11, the Dragon glyph is in house 12 and the Wind glyph is in house 13.

This can be charted as follows:

13 Moon Mayan cross of Mister James Redfield

THE "ORIGIN" GLYPH
OR "BIRTHGUIDE"
GLYPH

THE SUN

THE ANTIPODE OR CHALLENGE GLYPH

THE DOG

THE IDENTITY OR BIRTH GLYPH OR KIN

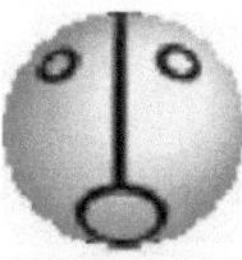

THE SUN
KIN 180

THE ANALOGUE OR ALLY GLYPH

THE STORM

THE OCCULT OR DESTINATION GLYPH

THE DRAGON

DREAMSPELL OR EVOLUTIONARY PATH

Traditional calendar with GMT 584283 constant

Identity glyph:

Table 6: Constant for the year 1950 = 249
Table 7: Constant for the 19th of March = 258.

Total=507. You take away 260 when the total exceeds 260.
507-260=**247.**

Table 8: Kin 247 is « The Earth» with a tonality of 13.
The Identity glyph is therefore Earth with a tonality of 13.

Origin glyph: Origin glyph = Identity glyph - 8.
247 – 8 = 239

Glyph 239 on Table 8 is the Moon glyph with a tonality 5.

Feminine or Ally glyph: Ally glyph= Identity glyph + 6.

247 + 6 = 253

Glyph 253 on Table 8 is the Night glyph with a tonality of 6.

Masculine or challenge glyph: Ally glyph = Identity glyph -6.

247-6=241

Glyph 241 on Table 8 is the Monkey glyph with a tonality of 7.

Destination glyph: Destination glyph = Identity glyph +8.

247+8=255. Glyph 255 on Table 8 is the Snake glyph with a tonality of 8.

Evolutionary path, enchanted path or Dreamspell: When you go back from tonality 13 to tonality 1, you arrive at glyph number 235, the Snake glyph with a tonality of 1. You therefore obtain the evolutionary path of the Snake. This means the Snake glyph is in house 1, the Death or Bridge glyph is in house 2, the Deer or Hand glyph is in house 3, the Star glyph is in house 4, the Moon glyph is in house 5, the Dog glyph is in house 6, the Monkey glyph is in house 7, the Road glyph is in house 8, the Bamboo glyph is in house 9, the Jaguar glyph is in house 10, the Eagle glyph is in house 11, the Owl or Vulture or Warrior glyph is in house 12 and the Earth glyph is in house 13. On the website: http://www.pauahtun.org/cgi-bin/gregmaya.py you can see that the Lord of the night is G9. This can be charted as follows:

Traditional calendar Mayan cross of Mister James Redfield

THE "ORIGIN" GLYPH OR "BIRTHGUIDE" GLYPH

MULUK-THE MOON-5

THE ANTIPODE OR CHALLENGE GLYPH

BATZ- THE MONKEY-7

THE IDENTITY OR BIRTH GLYPH OR KIN

CABAN- THE EARTH - 13
KIN 247

THE ANALOGUE OR ALLY GLYPH

AKBAL-THE NIGHT OR HOUSE-6

THE OCCULT OR DESTINATION GLYPH

Lord of the night

G9

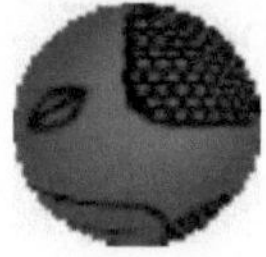

CHICCHAN-THE SNAKE-8

SNAKE DREAMSPELL

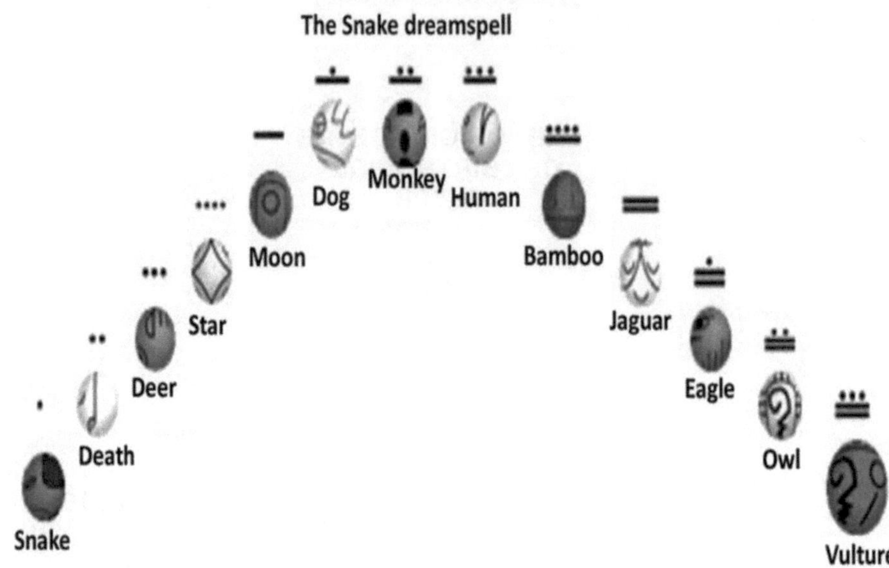

Traditional calendar with the VMR 774080 constant

You have a calculator on the website http://www.pauahtun.org/cgi-bin/gregmaya.py where you must input 774080 as conversion constant. You can also use table 9 in the appendices with tables 7 and 8 as before.

When you input 19th of march 1952 as the birth date and 774080 as the conversion constant, you get Kin 250 which is the Sun with a tonality of three as the Identity glyph and G4 as Lord of the night. If you apply the same procedure as with the traditional calendar, you will then find the Mayan cross and Trecena as below.

Third Mayan cross of Mister James Redfield

**THE "ORIGIN" GLYPH
OR "BIRTHGUIDE"
GLYPH**

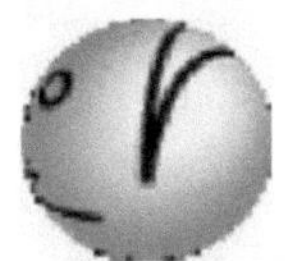

EB-THE HUMAN-8

**THE ANTIPODE OR
CHALLENGE
GLYPH**

IX-THE MAGICIAN-6

**THE IDENTITY OR
BIRTH GLYPH OR KIN**

**AHAU-THE SUN-3
KIN 250**

**THE ANALOGUE
OR ALLY GLYPH**

CIMI-DEATH-8

**THE OCCULT OR
DESTINATION GLYPH**

Lord of the night

G4

LAMAT-THE STAR-11

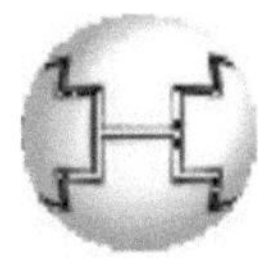

DREAMSPELL

THE MIROR

The Flint or Mirror dreamspell

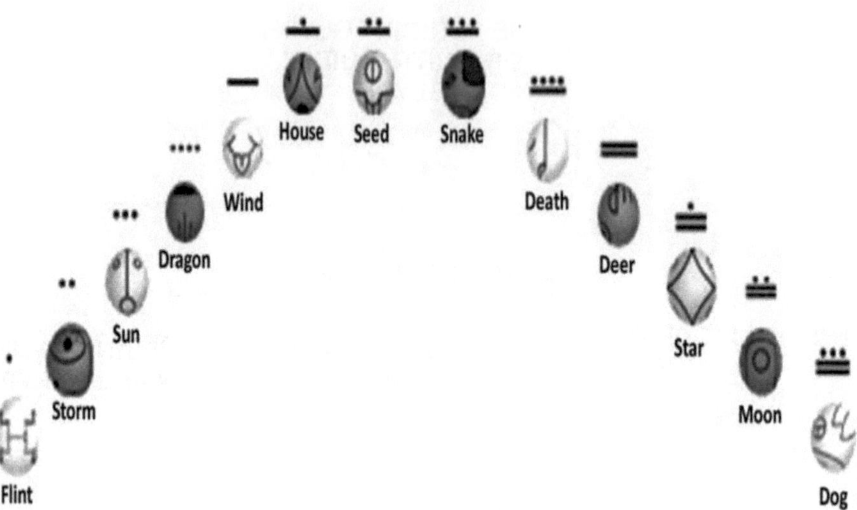

THE MESSAGES GIVEN BY THE TWENTY SACRED GLYPHS

1: THE DRAGON OR CROCODILE OR ALIGATOR

The Dragon is the original matrix represented by the Milky Way and the initial fire source of all life. It is the energy and motivation that sets life in motion. It puts an end to ignorance and starts a new cycle. It nourishes life by supplying what is necessary for life to advance. It lives intensively in the present moment, triggers actions and brings about confidence, faith and belief in abundance. It is represented by a rising sun's rays and seven seeds.

The Dragon symbolizes the tree of life that plunges its roots into the memories of the world. It is the very beginning, birth, Mother Nature who creates life through a life force that nourishes by supplying energy and motivation.

The Dragon represents that wisdom that exists since the beginning of time, the oldest memories from life before life and the gateway to knowledge. It brings the gift that allows you to just be who you are, in total silence, in total faith and confidence, fully in the present moment, without any thoughts or any fear, in a state of complete letting go while being always on the move, fully alive. It flies freely in the air and spits fire when necessary. Its fire power can be creative but also destructive if it is not channeled properly.

It has the power to create beginnings. It is like an inner fire that can start things up. It pushes you to act so as to get started. Its mission is to bring to life, to create and to start beings, groups, projects and undertakings but also to maintain them, to nourish them and to take care of them so that they can develop.

A Dragon who is connected with his spiritual essence is « life and action ». He knows how to shake himself up, how to let himself flare up through the power of love, how to use his ability to decide efficiently, how to control his eagerness and impatience, how to entertain his self-confidence and faith in life as well as a healthy and vigorous body by nourishing himself correctly in all domains, how to be assertive though life, action and an active life and how to follow the drives of his soul. He helps people get started, puts them on their spiritual paths, on the pathway that returns to "The Source". A sleeping Dragon is quite lazy. He starts a lot of things that he never finishes, is very impatient and waists his energy and his time.

This glyph invites you to dive into the depths of life's origin and to seek true nourishment, that nourishment which you need to evolve and that is lacking. You can obtain it by being receptive and confident, by choosing the right moment to act, by undertaking even if you have no guarantees of success and by setting yourself in motion without trying to control results. Receptivity and striking force are two of your major qualities.

Have faith in the guide that dwells within your heart. Allow him to lead you and have faith in the transformation process. Become aware that your true nature is unconditional love and show compassion. You can observe that at first, people often tend to try and control everything, change everything and improve their environment. You can then learn to accept what is and to just let things be as they are and follow their natural course.

The Dragon is telling you not to complain when it rains but on the contrary to cherish falling water and to accept the situation as it is. The Dragon is like a tree observing the surrounding world without Jugement and without wanting to change anything. And it become obvious that the time for action has come, he then acts efficiently.

By focusing on this feeling of obviousness, you can increase your confidence in yourself and believe more and more in the divine force of life. You can develop this special faith in life and become aware that the universe always answers your demands. It is essential to accepts life's gifts and to allow others to give to you and by being receptive and then by giving, you allow love to flow in your life.

If you connect yourself with the source of all life and creation, with the Universal Mother of life, you will have all the necessary resources to take care of others and of yourself. And you are very good at taking care of others and at protecting them. See if you are being overly protective and if you have a tendency to sacrifice yourself in order to nourish and help others. Don't be obsessed by your territory and don't try to dominate others as this would only nourish a feeling of being unsafe. Remember that you are in the hands of life and that Life has created you. Have faith that life and the world will continue to nourish you and to give you what is necessary for your journey.

If you feel that you lack help, consider going into your deep self, open up to the connection with the Source, prepare to receive abundance of life and act by following your intuition. Being confident means that there are no errors and no victims, just experiences, teachings and growth processes. Feel that you deserve to receive when others give to you and believe in the unlimited power of chance. It's up to you to ask for help to materialize and achieve your projects and your creations if such help is necessary.

Promote your talents and your integrity. Listen to your feelings, to your desires and to your dreams. Cherish your life as it is and act to place yourself in the flow of life. Be your own nourishing mother. Be aware of what you nourish within yourself and give yourself what you need. You can then nourish others. Observe where you put your attention, where energy flows in your life and within you and where it does not. Observe what gives you energy and what takes energy away from you.

By channeling energy and creative power and thanks to your intense presence and to your ability to tap into the collective subconscious and into what's in the air, you can bring about, within yourself and within others, new ideas, new projects and a new cycle.

2 – THE WIND THAT BRINGS RAIN OR THE BREATH OF LIFE.

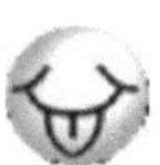 

Divine breath, voice that inspires words and songs, celestial messenger, power of the creative verb, the wind occupies space, sets life in motion and brings messages so as to reveal the original cosmic order, the truth and the « spirit » of what exists beyond all duality. It symbolizes trees, intelligence, communication, spreading out and adaptation.

The Wind or Ik represents the God Quetzalcoatl. It is the power of verb, the breath of life and of spirit. It is breathing. It is the power behind the movement of natural cycles. It acts to make communication exist using speech but also to give a spiritual meaning to every experience. With the Wind in your chart, you love communicating and you have the ability to give the right people the right information at the right time. You can spread positive ideas, be like a journalist or someone who transmits spirituality through communication.

A Wind who is connected with its spiritual essence and who is awake is well rooted in life and has great curiosity. He spreads truths coming from the breath of the Great Spirit. While being capable from seeing things from a distance, he is fully involved, very mobile, always flexible and adapts to whatever comes up. His speech is precise, relevant, just and inspired by the heart. He sets all life in motion. A sleeping Wind is a person who talks a lot and who makes a lot of noise but without any meaning or deepness and without transmitting anything. Such a person does not really succeed in communicating or in adapting.

This glyph invites you to open up your consciousness so as to live guided and inspired. It is asking you to get out of your thinking mind which means that you are not thinking all the time and that you are not continuously nourishing an internal dialogue. It is asking you to simplify, to listen, to be fully present in your body and to flow along your life path with truth, without playing games and without lying to yourself.

 It is asking you to be like the wind, spontaneous and open to change. It is asking you to take into account invisible forces that are in motion to guide you, inspire you and help you. Communicate what you feel, what is inside you and what you think with others. If you don't do so, you not only deprive yourself of being relieved from negative tension but also from feeling great pleasure. It is very important that you pay attention on how you communicate and that you avoid hurting others. Communicate from your heart and make sure love guides you. Avoid thoughts or words without love. Become aware that when you want, you are connected with your divine self. Express your potential and pay attention to inspirations that are been showed to you by your divine self.

You can also pay attention to any feelings of separation, abandonment or confinement and remember that a part of you is always connected to the Source of all life. The Wind is asking you to be an emissary of the great change that is coming on Earth so that everyone can live in a better world, in a world that is more harmonious, where everyone feels in peace and surrounded by love. Observe and study this feeling of separation. Observe that life never abandons you if you don't abandon it. Learn to feel the soft and happy feeling of reunification and of being connected to life. Leaning to breathe consciously can greatly help to experience such feelings. Try breathing slowly and deeply until you can notice that there is no more separation between the air in motion, your lungs in motion and the person who is breathing, as if life was breathing through you.

Learn to use the magical energy of words, by choosing words and sentences that raise you and move you, by repeating them on a daily basis, by learning to feel the words until you feel yourself as the consciousness of the words chosen, until it feels like it is the words that speak you and not you who speaks the words, until the words become alive within you and until your soul unites with these living words. Find your way of communicating with others, wether through speech, writing, action or though a profession. Become aware that you are able to communicate what's best in you. What is most important is that you learn to experiment the connection with the divine self by acting according to your inspirations, by feeling the reunifying presence of the Great Spirit and then by communicating clearly.

It is of great importance that you communicate what you feel correctly, that you avoid wounding others and that you listen to what others have to say concerning breathing and communication. Your speech then become amazingly clear, precise, relevant, inspired by your heart and sets life in motion.

3 – NIGHT OR HOME OR THE SOURCE OF ABUNDANCE

Night symbolizes an inner journey in invisible worlds and into the mysterious. It symbolizes the creation and the exploration of one's sanctuary, one's home. It reveals the gifts and richness of the subconscious amongst which is the magical power of true faith. In the world of dreams and then in the world of matter, the coming together of male and female principles concentrates energy to create, protect and regenerate life and then to make one's dreams, one's abundance and one's personal power expressed and come true. With the Night glyph, every talent and all of one's potential can be expressed. The glyph is represented by two veils that are being moved apart.

Night represents the exploration of what is invisible, of secrets, of dreams and of one's inner world. It allows you to confront your dark zones and to bring them to light. It creates dawn and a new birth. Its main tool is active intuition. Night is the guardian of the house and of the home where one recharges one's batteries by nourishing oneself.

The first goal of the Night glyph is to create and protect a happy home where every member of the family can recharge himself. Night protects home, family and wellness by keeping dark elements out.

The second goal of the Night glyph is to help you create abundance in your life. This abundance is made up of both material and spiritual elements. To generate it, it is necessary to nourish a clear intention, to find and nourish joy in your heart, to communicate and to organize yourself efficiently and practically using the power of true faith. See that joy and action are abundances nourishments.

The Night glyph tunes you in with vacuity and with the matrix of creation, this special zone of reality where things are not yet manifested but where everything potentially exists. From there, you have the ability to create abundance in matter by finding new ideas, artistic inspirations, intuitions and organized solutions. Night is the hidden and secret place, the mysterious place where the Great Spirit creates abundance in life. The Night glyph invites you to sit in silence and to dive into darkness, in your inner vacuity, in total quietness, without any fear, any expectations or any thoughts until you feel yourself like a very happy egg shaped luminous liquid and then to go in the world of dreams so as to experiment spiritual vision.

The space and time of dreams carries many opportunities. Take a close look at your dreams because treasures are hidden within them. There, you will discover your talents, your potential, your dreams, your soul plan, your ideas and your joy. Enter your dreams where everything is possible, where there is no difference between the future and the present, between what you believe and what you hope for.

See that true faith is not believing in something you know to be true because you have experienced it but that it is an inner feeling of certainty that you will get or reach what your faith promises and above all that you have the strength and power to do what must be done. See that your faith receives the forces of your will, just as a mould receives content. It then creates a new form with what it has received, an event or an object, that is materializes into your life. You can hereby bring to life, from your inside to the real world, the necessary elements to create achievements according to your soul plan.

This glyph invites you to use your faith to put your dreams and desires into shape and to express them in the real world according to your faith. It invites you to create your personal dream. You may also experience telepathic connections during your dreams, where you can receive messages and information. Night is also the power of intuition and night vision.

When it is dark and when one cannot see anything, other senses come into action. When you are spiritually connected and when you combine your mental power with your intuition, you can become a master of intuition, a seer, a teller, a tarologist or a coach who is like a light guiding people in darkness, in the night of matter. You can help other people see clearly their life paths and bring light, through clarity and understanding, to the dark zones hidden in the individual unconscious self.

A sleeping Night can either create a lack of material prosperity or greediness and consumerism or either a permanent feeling of anguish, uncertainty and insecurity. If you observe that somewhere in your life, you are limited by some internal process or by a specific problem, instead of resisting or creating anguish, look within yourself, globally observe what is happening, examine your beliefs, your memories and your thoughts. See how you judge yourself, assess yourself and prevent yourself from getting access to your natural joy. Remember that those beliefs that are ready to be changed first come closer and closer to your consciousness through the path of darkness. They then pop up in your consciousness so that you can deal with them. Take care of them and be ready to go into the unknown, deep within, in your inner sanctuary, to find the talents and treasures that are waiting there for you. You will encounter great potentials, beautiful gifts and a great joy. All these are only waiting for you to be expressed so that your growth can be successful.

4 – THE SEED OR MAIZE STEM OR THE LIZARD

The seed contains, in a very small unit, all the information and programs necessary for evolution. It shows that every project starts with a simple idea. It enables finding the ground and the appropriate conditions so that all the information contained in the seed can be expressed though action, so that the life program it carries can thrive and so that awareness can blossom. To go from a seed to a maize stem or to a tree is a large scale project that can only succeed when there is an efficient organization, distribution and management of resources, energy and information, slowly but steadily. A seed handles projects, works to make resources bear fruit so as to perpetuate life and guides people who travel in the invisible regions of life. It is firmly rooted in earth while turned towards the sky and sunlight, thus connecting ideals and practical life. All potentials can come through with the Seed glyph.

The Seed is the germ of life. It represents fertility, sensuality and creative sexual energy. It carries in itself all the possibilities that will exist in the future, all desires and all potential projects. It symbolizes evolution's organized growth and ordering power that takes place through the blossoming of though forms and of the idea of who you are, through the revelation of a potential and of a genetic code, from the Source where every human being comes from. The Seed symbolizes organized action, potential projects, an impulse to blossom and to experience fulfillment, an impulse to saw so as to reap later on as well as a power to grow and develop.

The Seed glyph represents the seed in itself, the fertile ground where it can grow thanks to appropriate nutriments but also the network to which it belongs. The Seed communicates with the world though its five senses.
It is a symbol of Mother Nature that is undertaking to make numerous projects come to life. It is a bundle of joy that happily wants to become a beautiful plant. So should you be. Just like the Seed, you are attracted to the light of your divine essence which invites you to thrive and blossom so that all your potential may be expressed and so that your true divine nature may be revealed. To help individuals and communities blossom, the Seed reveals what is needed secrets and hidden disappointments.

It allows you to become free from past beliefs, from past limiting influence and from what no longer needs to be so that everyone can become a new person.

An enlightened Seed know when it's time to talk and when it's time to be silent, when to saw and when to harvest. It is able to express courage and gratitude. It is able to make situations and people blossom in a way that seems magical. Its mission is to teach and to help people's Spirits blossom by helping them to grow, mature and fulfill. The Seed is very good at handling projects because it has great capabilities to use data efficiently and to coordinate a network of people.

A sleeping Seed does nothing to blossom, does not understand the laws of the universe and lives a very limited life, gradually fading away in sadness.

A Seed needs water and light to grow and so do you. It needs to be connected with other Seeds so as to be part of a greater whole. Water symbolizes emotions and fluidity that follows the path of least resistance. Light symbolizes consciousness, awareness, creative power and gratitude.

Seek those emotions that uplift you and the light of consciousness so that you talents and your potential can germinate and blossom.

Learn to meditate in total silence to see where and when light has difficulty entering into your consciousness. You are your own field of investigation. Leave darkness behind you and allow yourself to become the gift of life that you really are. Lear to appreciate the gifts that are given to you and to grasp the teachings and lessons brought to you by life. Mystery blossoms in you thanks to the power of your intentions, of your thoughts and of what you nourish.

Maybe you have a tendency to be static so as to be protected and safe in your shell or bubble and so as not to feel vulnerable. Observe how you limit your own growth. Break this shell made of ideas, memories, limiting beliefs and mental structures to which you are attached. Undertake so as to become free from those beliefs that give you a feeling of safety and bring new possibilities of growth into your life.

You are also like a receptive Earth and your desires naturally attract the help you need. All your dreams and desires spread about within you and hope to be one day awakened and brought to life so that though them you can blossom. Plant your intentions. They will know how to guide you towards their achievement. See and feel that it is possible for your dreams to come true and allow them to emerge.

You are a sower and a harvester. Become aware of your dreams and of your deep aspirations. Imagine that they can be achieved in the world if you help them. This glyph is inviting you to plant a seed though an intention, a project or a dream, depending on what your heart tells you and then to work on the ground all around while being receptive so that things may blossom. Take the time factor into account and act rightly. The seed knows when it is the right time to pop out of the earth. There is a time to sow, a time for waiting, a time for growing and a time for reaping. Realize yourself where you have the potential to do so.

As you move along though your different learning phases and life phases, you saw different desires and different intentions. As your growth patterns become clear, your awareness of your deep inner truth gradually turns into wisdom and becomes one with the world of light where all seeds blossom. There is then no more difference between you and between what, in appearance, is not you. When your sow your personal deep inner truth, there is more truth on planet Earth.

You are the able to find adequate solutions thanks to your intelligence of life. You are able to create more and more fertile grounds where you can express who you are, in harmony with nature and with the flow of life.

Handle your spiritual path like a project. Give yourself the means to flourish, to blossom and to prosper in a state of joy and communion. You can then connect with others and help them to blossom and prosper.

Your real self can be compared to a luminous seed created by the source of all life. This seed is currently asleep or in the dark because your awareness is no longer there. This seed is made of a body and of a hollow part in its center. When you become the image of the best of who you are and then the best of yourself, when you learn to feel yourself as a luminous and happy liquid inside the center of yourself, thanks to the power of love, faith and work on yourself so as to free yourself, you allow this seed to welcome once again in its center a luminous spiritual sacred spark that comes from the galactic center, from the source of all life. The sleeping seed you once were then becomes once again the body of this luminous sacred spark. You then experience a rebirth inside this new spiritual body and become once more like a luminous tree or like a radiating being that shines very brightly as it is reconnected with the source of all life.

5 – THE SNAKE

The snake symbolizes the primitive mind that is capable of feeling and seeing the invisible energy that exists here and now, of generating a powerful life force, of satisfying essential needs and of adapting in a fluidic manner even in difficult conditions. The fire of life in matter is expressed through the snake. It expresses a cosmic life force that always moves forward, a sure instinct that initiates the right action, an awareness of eternity, a survival instinct and the ability to master energy. It represent the energy, also called Kundalini, that flows in the backbone and in the Chakras or energy centers in the body, allowing a person to be connected to both earth energy and sky energy. The snake teaches you how to use and express the body as a means to bring about change and how to make sexual energy flow harmoniously so as to bring about as much vitality as possible.

The Snake's energy allows the human race to reproduce itself and nature to exist. The Snake symbolizes fighting spirit as an impulse to live and survive. It symbolizes physical growth, sexuality and mastering subtle energies.

It is a force that is aware of its uniqueness and that is also capable of going from ignorance to knowledge and from darkness to light, thanks to an ability to experience mysteries and motion of energy within the body.

Thanks to his very strong struggling instinct and a lot of life force, the Snake can channel his energy in any intensive activity, in any activity requiring a lot of physical strength and resistance to wear down and in any activity which is a test to the survival instinct. The Snake is closely connected to his body and to nature. It has a strong ecological awareness and feels concerned about preserving species. A sleeping snake tends to nourish a tendency not to accept people and situations as they are. It tends to reject people and to be afraid of being betrayed, which tends to make him want to control everything. It then becomes depressive and a victim of his saboteur. It gets intoxicated by violent emotions, by relationships based on dependency and by aggressive or destructive behavior and tends to channel his energy mainly through sex without love or through negative thoughts.

An enlightened and awakened Snake is incredibly lucid and vigilant. It is highly flexible and adapts to all situations.
It seeks to experiment light with all its strength and to dive into vacuity until it reaches the space where light exists beyond darkness so as not to remain in darkness.

It becomes aware that there is a slippery and uncertain path, that leads to darkness and maintains one in darkness and misery, and another path that is narrow and solid as rock, that leads to light and happiness. It learns to avoid situations where there is an energetic, financial and emotional dependency. It learns to see that the power that maintains one in a state of slavery is based on ignorance, untrue beliefs, fears and on a misplaced focus of attention. It learns to go away from such power and from shining mirages that seek to attract attention and to reject anything that does not enable a radiating expression of love and a long lasting serenity.

It is aware that hatred is the opposite force of love, that it is a refuge for those who have no power, that it is a force that has not yet discovered its power and that hatred must be transformed into love and creative power in order to free itself. It learns to despise hatred, to avoid focusing its attention on it and nourishing it as it knows how miserable it makes a person. It therefore acts to express the best of itself, develops its power and uses it to serve life.

Because it knows how to synchronize his desires with what his heart needs, with his life power and because he knows how to maintain a high intensity vibratory state, he is capable of transforming everything in a way that seems just like magic.

It allows experiencing the miracles and wonders of the human body with its vitality. It connects earth and sky, the heart and the body, by combining authority and truth, to bring justice on earth, through a sincere willingness to serve others.

The Snake gives you the life force and awareness to act intuitively and instinctively at each moment, to let your feelings bring solutions to existing problems and to listen to what your body and your instincts have to say in the present moment. This helps you to become free from old mental patterns.

The snake also helps you put aside fears and inferior desires and to experience detoxination, purification and transformation processes.

It gives you the intuition, the sensuality, the passion and the fighting spirit to let your creative power express itself and to control situations. Listen carefully to the messages given by your body and your intuition as in them can be found the path that shows you what must be done in each situation. Lear to feel that with a healthy sexuality and intimacy awakens your vitality and passion for life.

Do your best to avoid living a boring life by taking a good look at your behavior and your habits. Try to feel what is right and to find new paths that bring more spontaneity and emotion. Try not to grant so much attention to your physical body and to how other people see you.

 Learn to see that the only positive and beneficial sexual relationships are those that occur with love within a long lasting relationship and that your ultimate goal exists within the light at the center of your heart. Use your body as a tool for your inner transformation. Explore your feelings, your sensations, your emotions and above all the vibrations that you perceive as a way to become more aware of who you are. By becoming aware of the flow of life force within you, you can experiment the sacred fire of the Snake's dance that takes place within you.

From the light of love that comes out of your heart, feel your sexual energy, the flow of energy in your body and your emotions as energies that will set you free, by allowing you to choose at every moment what is right for you and by enabling you to feel what the appropriate solution is. You can this way become an enlightening device and a transformation tool at the service of life.

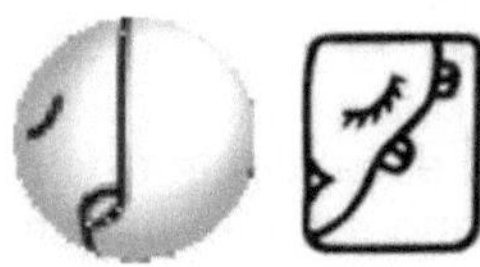

The Bridge enables you to perceive yourself and others in their eternal essence, to leave behind what is ancient and what is no longer of use and to change your vision so as to become free from patterns and beliefs that impede happiness. It enables you to transform yourself and others, to connect worlds between themselves and to experience initiation so as to become reborn to your deep inner truth. Life implies permanent change which means abandoning what no longer needs to be and seeing death as a threshold that must be crossed to bring about renewal.

Thanks to a clear vision of the beginnings of cycles and of the end of cycles, the World Bridger can master the time and space existing between the two while letting go of any tendency to try and control everything. It can generate the healing energy that brings about renewal. He can build bridges between people and situations and transcend any fear of death.

This glyph symbolizes the power of death and transformation, guided by the power of the heart that has transcended fear. It represents life, death and renewal cycles and ancestral memories. It is like a bridge that is capable of communicating between two worlds, by contacting and connecting with other dimensions of life. It is the bridge who contacts ancestors in life hereafter so as to get help. It is the bridge who transcends death by showing us that it is just a simple crossing over and just a simple changing of frequency. The Bridge has the ability to open certain doors and to close others.

The Bridge is able to relax completely, to focus inwards, to observe intensively and to call the light by creating a silent space within and then to dive into the darkness inside himself along an invisible bridge that leads him to the luminous space at the center of his heart and then to go to the other side of the bridge by transferring his consciousness inside his light body. The Bridge is then the one who dies to become reborn, who painlessly leaves behind him what is ancient and ignorance so as to naturally welcome what is new. He is therefore capable of giving up a job, old rancors and sufferings, past history, love stories that no longer exist and above all ego with all the fiction that goes with it. He can then get access to a state of grace brought by the superior self and become a bridge between the "Source of all life" and Men.

An enlightened Bridge is an organizer, a transformer, a guide and a healer. He is capable of quietly guiding souls though times of change and through transition periods by reconnecting each person to his deep inner truth. In daily life he is very good at public relations because he connects people together. With this glyph, it is essential that you understand the process of the physical body's death and of the transformation of matter and to consider such processes as natural means for growth. It is essential that you learn "the art of dying" by just being always ready to die and to leave everything behind you, with joy and serenity. It is also vital that you become aware of your connections with your ancestors and that these connections have of the power to influence you and your life. If you don't do so, you may have to go through pain and suffering because of a tendency to sabotage your life and to get tied up in a victim's role. Before getting access to new paths, you must abandon the old ones and get rid of whatever is a burden for you.

Ask yourself if your possessions, your situation, your relationships, your ideas, your beliefs and your judgments serve your growth or on the contrary if they prevent you from going forward and growing. You will be placed in situations where you have to let go, to abandon what is no longer necessary and to forgive but possibly also situations where you feel your body vibrating because you need to experiment what is called "out of body experiences". Any resistance results from a fear of death that you must overcome. You must realize that you are not really living as long as you don't see death as a consequence of life and until you are not fully aware of your ancestral memories. Death is nothing more than a thin barrier behind which hides another reality. You must therefore let go without fear and forgive what must be thanks to the power of your heart.

This glyph is also asking you to stop seeking perfection and to stop trying to control everything. It is asking you to become free from any expectations and from artificially created ideas as to how things and people should be, to forgive yourself and others, to abandon old angers that limit your evolution and your possibilities so as to live in a much more inspired manner. By abandoning what is limiting you, you allow yourself to experience, symbolically, death. This symbolic death allows you to create space for new ideas, new encounters, new relationships and a new life. You hereby allow your true being to emerge and you can discover your deep inner truth.

You can then use your organizing abilities, your talents to do trade or business, your ability to guide people in times of change and your ability to build bridges between people, things, information or groups to serve your community. Mayans believed that days corresponding to this glyph where lucky days for trade and chance.

A clear vision on how people, things and information can work well together leads to a technical, artistic, manual, energetical and healing intelligence. This enables seeing how a person becomes one with their ideas or knowledge, being open to all knowledge, being capable of weighing the correctness of any information and adapting to the surrounding world through a clever management of data systems, organization, coordination and relationships. The will achieves goals through permanent and appropriate movement of information. The Hand can know, do, materialize, improve and heal with great wisdom. It leads to the true path of knowledge though experience and action and through an awareness of the great value of well done work. The glyph is symbolized by a hand and by the ring belonging to the village's sage or healer.

The Hand is a gateway that opens access to the understanding and knowledge of other dimensions. It closes a cycle and opens the way to a new cycle and a new state of being. It brings an intuitive understanding of the new world. This new world is life in motion where wisdom, beauty and intelligence (spirituality, art and science) are harmoniously combined together. Seeing and understanding the beauty of life in motion can allow you to express yourself though dancing or art as the Hand enables you to dance your life and to see the beauty in all things. This requires being centered in your personal power and to see your own beauty. From there, beauty naturally expresses itself through you and you ego tunes into divine will. Your presence then invites each person to express their deep inner truth and to be who they really are.

The Hand glyph carries various talents. It can heal the body's and soul's wounds. It can make wishes come true and materialize in everyday life. It can fix things and produce objects. Manual or spiritual talents can be expressed though you. These talents and qualifications are nourished by a practical intuition and by an intuitive understanding of people, things and of life and its cycles. The Hand glyph is also connected to the power of touch and to the vision of how forms and materials can work out. From there comes an understanding of form, an ability to support and hold, to help, to heal, to act and to create things with one's hands. The hand glyph also helps one maintain a healthy body and soul through intuitive knowledge and through an ability to produce objects. Because of this concern for health and because of this ability to heal, many people carrying this glyph are healers, doctors, vets, psychologists, therapists, physiotherapists, people who do massage or who use alternative therapies.

Knowing is one of the key words for the Hand glyph. The Hand gets to know about things because it is extremely curious about everything, and particularly about everything concerning knowledge of the body, of plants or of spirituality. It doesn't like not knowing and not being able to control or do something about it. The Hand glyph wants to know intuitively. Strongly devoted to others, is can easily put aside its own interests to spend all its time taking care of others. The path of the Hand glyph is to combine the use of personal power with humbleness, understanding and service to others.

An awakened Hand works all the time and serves humanity all the time. It loves life, is very generous and very smart. It can create all the necessary tools to adapt to the world of matter and to improve people's life. People with this glyph work a lot because they know that intense and well done work renews one's own strength. A sleeping hand tends to always feel sick or unwell, is unable to heal itself or others, serves no one, doesn't take care of itself and is always complaining. It then becomes a victim of its own intelligence and wastes its time and energy.

Take good care of your hands and let them do what they want to do. Do they want to work with earth? Do they want to write, draw, garden, create things, do some manual work, dance or do massage? Very creative activities connected with healing can take place though your hands. The Hand glyph gives you the power of achievement and a natural tendency to go towards what is new. It brings you an open mindedness that enables you to receive and use spiritual or material tools and techniques which can heal or interact with people in new ways. It enables you to free yourself and others from any energy, emotional or physical block and therefore to have access to your talents, gifts and qualifications. There are certainly talents and gifts to develop within you as well as new ways to consider your life. It's up to you to go through the doors that show up. This glyph's dark side can be an excessive tendency to seek perfection, a difficulty to finish things or a tendency to delay things to later on. The Hand glyph makes one want to be capable and to see real results of the work done. Observe yourself and see if you resist, if you put too much pressure on yourself, if you take to many different directions at once or if you lose yourself in distractions. Have confidence in your potential and in those talents that seek to be expressed by you, even if you don't see results right away. Find satisfaction in every step of your path and fill in the gaps in your life as best you can. You have all the capabilities to achieve what you want to. You just have to dare go through the door that will bring you to the achievement of your aspirations and desires. You can then use your hands, your talents, your knowledge and your intuition to experience a harmonious relationship with the universe and to serve others. Remember that life is using you as its tool to serve.

8: VENUS OR THE STAR OR THE RABBIT

The star glyph, which is actually the planet Venus, brings the connection and sensitivity to the beauty and harmony that exists in nature, in what seems to be chaos of form and expression and also in the underlying order behind all that lives. This can be expressed through all forms of art, through the use of the senses and through a strong awareness of the order of things. The Star generates creative power and joy, pleasure and harmony. It makes reality more beautiful by creating forms everywhere, in all directions. It enables you to enjoy both material and spiritual pleasures. It invites you to leave behind you anything that takes you away from joy, harmony or beauty so as to create happiness on Earth and so as to make your life, with wisdom, a piece of art.

Light made of love, the Star glyph symbolizes light embodied in matter. It is the power of love taking shape, the beauty of the great cosmic evolution plan and beauty within matter. It is the force that reveals harmony that unites everything. It brings a talent to understand form and color and to create harmony. It also brings aesthetic skills, social intelligence, ethics, simplicity and awareness of limits. It can out pass everything though beauty.

It enables reproducing and multiplicating in order to generate abundance. It finally brings that special touch of grace and beauty that makes things so previous. It symbolizes inner harmony that generates harmony in the outside world. With the Star, creation becomes an art that brings beauty in the world. The Star enables you to embellish, to create forms, to bring things to their perfection and to finish creations so that they can become works of art. The Star attracts luck and enables sharing with others in a state of joy.

The Star can give natural abilities for writing, painting, art, music, dance, massage, architecture, decoration, design and to be connected with the planets and the stars. A sleeping Star feels frustrated and unsatisfied, usually because it cannot channel its creative energy as it is so much focused on form, on the outside and not enough in its heart. This creates a mismatch between what the heart says and a need for pleasure.

Star people can then easily become too centered on a quest for pleasure and beauty, on others and on relationships and not enough on themselves and on their hearts. The dark side of the Star is a tendency to excessively seek perfection, to make confusion between evolution and perfection and to resist all the time. Star people may also encounter a difficulty to take themselves in charge, to be independent and autonomous in life and to take care of the evolution of their consciousness. Stars can only be seen when there is sufficient darkness. This glyph brings your soul plan, your evolution plan and the vision of your greatest potential. The Star invites you to awaken your attention, your ability to focus and your ability to contemplate yourself from a broader point of view. It invites you to take a leap of awareness towards a different way of seeing things, of listening to things and of being. It invites you to practice harmony on a daily basis and to convert this harmony into an essence that guides you in your life. That implies listening to your intuition, following what your heart says and abandoning any situation that limits your inner harmony.

It is possible that you live in a very limited or intellectual manner. Learn to be simple and free yourself from useless knowledge, judgments and a tendency to criticize. Become aware of your talents, of your gifts and of your ability to produce. You can then express through form all of these gifts and talents you have chosen, connect to the fullness of your beauty and express the harmony that emerges from within you by practicing the art of smiling and by creating harmonious relationships. This glyph also invites you to avoid seeking perfection and to stop expecting perfection in everything, in yourself or in others. It is asking you to let things be as they want to be so that things are fluid and harmonious.

Everything has its reason to exist and is part of a cosmic plan even if you do not see it that way. There are different levels of awareness, different levels of existence and different ways of seeing a specific situation. You possibly feel that there is only one path that is correct. Remember that you are the only one that has the answers you need. It depends only on you to integrate the knowledge you have acquired, to see the truth existing in all teachings and to create your own path so as to find your own wisdom and your own deep inner truth. This can lead to a high speed growth that connects you with your deep inner truth. From there emerges your inner beauty. Behave with love so as to put aside any disharmony that might come up in your life and synchronize yourself with universal harmony so as to embody grace. You can then spread it out where you go. Be autonomous and use you natural social intelligence to adapt. You have chosen this glyph to discover and practice harmony in every aspect of your life, to balance and harmonize everything that surrounds you and above all so that there is always pleasure and joy in your heart.

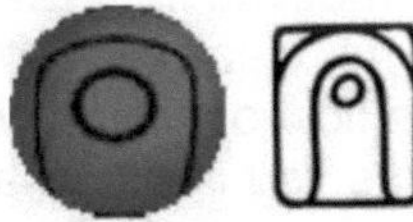

The moon is connected to life's natural fluidity. It represents the purification of the emotional body that to the motion of water and to work on emotions. It gives Earth water and food. It gives human beings intuition, emotion, sensitivity and imagination. It enables going from unwellness to wellness and it perpetuates life thanks to an emotional intelligence that creates fluidity and thanks to an ability to recharge one's batteries. The moon also represents the payment due to life by human beings, payment that can be paid by taking care of oneself, of life, of people and of the planet.

The Moon symbolizes universal water, the power to purify water and the energy of life that flows with fluidity. It symbolizes seas, rivers, water in the body, tears and sweat. All life needs water. Emotions are like water and the Moon is the queen of emotions.
It is capable of channeling emotional currents. It brings the strength of emotion, adaptability, balance and collective harmony.

Stagnant water becomes polluted. Certain emotions that you repress can also pollute your body and your soul. It's important that you let your emotions flow and that you observe your emotions without Jugement.

It would do you a lot of good to work with water, in a swimming pool, in a sauna or in the sea. It is also very important for you to drink enough water and to drink good quality water. You can filter your water and learn to reinform using words symbols or sounds so that it recovers its natural joy. It's also important that you learn to manage your emotions and that you nourish yourself with positive emotions.

When energy flows freely within you, you can easily feel your way through situations and people. You have a talent to feel how things are. You have a great emotional and intuitive intelligence. You have the ability to know what is true and what is false as you are like antennae that receives unsaid words. Because of your openness to intuition and because of your ability to channel and master the flow of emotions, you can strongly inspire other people's creative power and desires.

A "sleeping Moon" can be like a pack of ice with no emotions or on the contrary like an emotional tsunami. It can be depressive, apathetic, confined in its bubble and without any motivation. Water then invites you to purify yourself, to detoxify yourself, to clean up your past and your personal history and to reestablish a free flow of energy within you. It makes you very sensitive to cleanliness and turns you into a charming, pure, sincere, candid and innocent person.

Your task is to purify your whole being and in particular your emotions. You can also help others purify themselves, trigger people's creative power and help people experiment emotional freedom. The Moon also makes you capable of participating in collective undertakings, like a drop of water in the ocean, so that life can be perpetuated. The Moon is an antenna for cosmic awareness. By listening to your sensitivity, you can become more and more aware of the sighs sent to you by life. From there, you can take and adopt what really nourishes you and help others become aware of what truly nourishes them. Such signs are there for your personal growth by helping you see things more clearly along your path.

10 – THE DOG

The Dog is capable of seeing the worthiness and the merit of each person with fidelity and loyalty. He opens his heart so as to find a companion and share. He brings a feeling of belongingness as well as a gregarious or herd instinct. Always available to express his feelings and to love, he however needs quality and balance within a relationship to express his love. He connects with people, creates bonds and also expresses authority, both on a material and spiritual level. He hereby represents creation and application of law and the protection of territory.

The Dog symbolizes the emotional connection that enables sharing and that enables people to work together as a team. The Dog makes emotions and love flow by expressing his feelings. He represents the power of the heart, the power of unconditional love in all its diversity, the power of giving and of receiving, the power of sharing, of trusting and of loyalty. The Dog is the guardian of precious people whom he protects. He also represents authority and law.

He enables you to intimately connect, in a state of love, with others so as to create beautiful friendly, love or family relationships. The Dog also has the power to guide you and to show you which is the right way! What is currently guiding you? What is good for you? What are your dreams? What makes your heart happy and sing? Are you refusing to see something important to avoid confrontation with yourself or someone? These are all important questions for the Dog!

Dog people fulfill through love and by giving their lives to Life. They are naturally brave, warm hearted, loyal and faithful. They are also quite playful and know how to enjoy beautiful things in life. They love working in pairs, within a team and in a group rather than alone. Awakened Dog people constantly develop a will to make joy exist and learn to live in a state of joy. They recognize and acknowledge the power of love, allow themselves to be lit up by love and express the creative power of love in their daily lives. They then feel and express true unconditional love and are faithful to what they values. They learn to work on themselves so as to know how to handle their emotions and how to go beyond emotions that limit their spiritual growth. Dog people need variety in their work and in their lives and they need to work with people. They can be very good leaders because they know how to impose their views.

They can accomplish great deeds if they find the mission that fits them and that makes sense for them, even if they are not the original creator of the task, company or mission that they are involved in. Finding a mission that makes sense and where they can get involved is their greatest challenge. Have you found your mission?

A sleeping dog does not like himself and has no joy. He suffers from jealousy. He is not faithful to his divine self that is made of unconditional love. He tends to be obsessed by those whom he loves and to strongly attached to others when there is no spiritual opening. The Dog glyph invites you to pay great attention to the people that come along your path. These people arrive in your life to teach you what you need to learn and to reveal the different parts of yourself. Take a close look at the relationships you have with your friends, with your partner, with groups or with acquaintances and see what teachings they bring in your life. You may be here on Earth to take care of someone that needs your help, with faithfulness and loyalty which are ways of expressing love.

The more you express who you are in an authentic manner and the more you attract your true soul family and the people who can be your life companions. The more you pay attention to your dreams, the more you nourish them and the more they can come true. It is also important that you pay attention to the roles you play and to the roles and events that repeat themselves in an obsessional manner. The Dog glyph gives you the chance to clearly see your inside, your patterns and your memories and to avoid falling into intense emotional reactions that always lead to the same results. It would be very beneficial for you to see your emotional drama in a non passionate way, to become free from your personal history and from those emotions that are connected with it. You can do this by finding the teachings that reveal the roots that caused the events that are troubling you and by understanding why life has brought in your life the various people that are there.

Your ability to move around, to explore new places and to create new relationships will give you a great feeling of freedom. Every strong negative emotion comes from a non healed wound or from experiences that have not been understood and solved. Learn to accept what happened, do your best to see that, considering the personal history of the people involved, things could not have happened any other way and learn to forgive yourself and other people by calling upon the unconditional love that is within you. These encounters occurred to bring you certain teachings. There are no victims and it is now time to heal any unsettled matters so as to create space for renewal, for new perceptions and for new emotions. You can then connect yourself with your inner guide, with a faithful ally that guides you all the way along in your life and in particular during initiatic experiences. You can learn to master your life, love relationships, feelings and emotion. You can then become, on Earth, a messenger of natural joy and unconditional love. You can then guide people on the path of love and serve life.

11 – THE MONKEY OR CRAFTSMAN

The monkey is a time weaver and the force that dissolves illusions created by the always thinking mind between what was and what will be. It symbolizes the inner child that is always ready to play, the unpredictable, innocence, intelligence and spontaneity. It expresses itself through both an artistic, practical and business orientated way of thinking but also through playing, curiosity, sense of humor, movement and service, bringing along smiles and joy where it is. It can thus easily and playfully pass on messages and teachings. The Monkey is gifted to put masks on and to take them off. He has a chameleon like behavior and he knows how to create magic in the present moment by making people feel wonder.

For the Mayas, the Monkey was the time weaver who handled many strings at a time and who was capable of mixing new ideas, new concepts or new inventions on the web of reality so as to change our lives using the products of his never-ending, innocent and playful curiosity. The Monkey symbolizes the power of humor, of playing games and of a jack of all trades with many talents and capabilities.

He brings along the magic of every moment thanks to his spontaneity, to his ability to be in total unity with what is here and now and to his talent for improvisation. The Monkey has the gift of allowing himself to play, to enjoy life and to connect himself with the magic of every situation. It invites you to let go the fictions and illusions created by the ego and to welcome whatever life brings you, whatever it is.

Thanks to your natural charm and loveliness, to your pleasant humor, to your playfulness and to your sense of humor, you bring joy to your environment. The Monkey also represents the power of smart and practical intelligence, skill, agility and a talent from trade. An awakened Monkey is like a pure child expressing itself in the truth of what is. It clearly distinguishes between the mind with its intelligence and awareness and its spiritual energy. It knows that its intelligence is a wonderful tool and that it can never replace life and experience and it knows how to shut it up whenever it has no right to express itself.

It enjoys life at every moment, innocently. Using play, laughter and agility he is capable of seeing the divine essence and the magic existing in every person. It is capable of doing almost anything and it is gifted for buying and selling activities and for finding smart technical solutions to any difficulty.

A sleeping Monkey permits itself nothing and cannot concentrate on one same matter for very long. This prevents it from digging deep into things and into life. He thinks all the time, forgets to be aware in silence and believes that his intelligence is God. He moves around in many directions, has a tendency to err, doesn't know how to enjoy life or to have a good time with things always attracts other people's attention with his whims, his tricks and his nonsense and gradually becomes a sad person.

This glyph is inviting you to tell the truth, to let a lot of laughter fill up your life, to express your inner child, in a spontaneous and unpredictable manner, to observe what becomes free when you do so and to observe that funny things can happen anytime in your life and change everything.
The result can be chaotic and make you feel unsafe but remember that perfection exists in everything and that when barriers fall down one after the other, your divine essence can appear.

Live your dreams whatever they are and learn to feel and see everything as joyful and funny. Walk along the path of your lost innocence, take of one by one the layers of worries and memories and ask for your eternity and your integrity, for your eternal and joyful creative power. Ask for that faith and confidence is life that exists in the center of your heart. Remember that as a child of the Source, of the Creator of all that is, you don't have to prove or do or be anything but the simple presence of unconditional love.

The Monkey is asking you to look carefully at your inner child and to see where it might have been wounded by your parents, by people in society or by society's restrictions. Be aware of any defensive patterns or any aggressive emotional reactions you may have implemented to protect yourself and to heal your inner child. Express what emerges within you in the present moment knowing that the following steps will show up by themselves. Use your intelligence to learn and then to help others learn by themselves. Be vulnerable and authentic. Accept the events of your life with good humor! Allow your inner child to express itself without restrictions and when you do so, be prepared for magical results! Remember that laughter and humor are powerful healers! You can then develop wisdom based on a deep knowledge, based on experience, of what life truly is!

12- THE HUMAN OR THE JAW OR THE ROAD OF THE HERB

Gifted with a powerful psychological or technological intelligence, the Human knows how to create bonds and connections, how to create and use networks and how to use his resources and richness to bring about progress and to help people, by guiding other human beings, so that they can live free and happy. The Human accepts his humanity and builds his own path towards freedom. He is very different from the other glyphs in that he always uses his free will and his ability to choose intelligently, while taking other people's freedom and evolution into account. His ability to connect himself with the "Source" that created him enables him to see the right solutions and to make the right decisions, the ones that help him adapt to his environment, handle resources intelligently and help people heal.

The Human is the son of the « Creator ». In him is deposited cosmic intelligence in which lies the superior mind that brings progress. He has the privilege of being able to choose, of being able to use his free will and of being an intermediate between Heaven and Earth.

The person who knows how to use his or her free will wisely can be a receptor of Divine Will and give others very good advice, thus helping them to grow and mature, by opening the paths towards a better future. The Human can be a means of serving Cosmic Intelligence which makes life flow on and help people on their life paths. That is how you will accomplish your destiny.

Human people become aware of their actions so as to experiment their free will. They need to assimilate knowledge and experience by uniting them to love and to sensations as otherwise, they tend to focus excessively on information and on their always thinking mind and they get stuck in their thoughts. They need to learn that wisdom implies knowledge, experience and being connected in one's heart and that truth can only be found in a thoughtless silence and within the heart.

Human people feel strongly connected to the group, to their community, to humanity and to future generations. They often find the true meaning of their lives by undertaking for the good of humanity.
They can help people in distress, poor people, sick people, old people or confused people. They are usually simple, modest and quiet, and do not particularly value recognition. They are often aware of being intermediates between life and men.

If they are spiritually asleep, they can be good at giving advice to others at a certain level but they don't know how to deal with their body, their memories or their lives, or how to do something with their own free will. This can lead them into creating situations where they are dependant and addicted to something or someone. When Human people lack money, support or love, it means they are limiting themselves because they have not dealt with their personal history, because they nourish a feeling of superiority or inferiority or because they have not healed certain wounds.

To go beyond your limits and share with the rest of humanity, this glyph is asking you to make sure you have a healthy and vigorous body so that it may receive the energy of Cosmic Intelligence. The ability to express a superior intelligence allows you to choose, to choose to help or to do nothing, to talk or to remain silent, to choose light or darkness, to let yourself be guided by chaos or by Cosmic Intelligence.

Human people are often afraid of being influenced or of influencing others wrongly. What are your choices? According to what are they made? Who is influencing you and how? Do you let other people choose though indifference or though love? Are you able to make your own choices and to let others make theirs so as to influence according to Cosmic Law?

The Human glyph allows you to tune in to a cosmic flow of intelligence, to vibrate according to a certain frequency and to make your environment vibrate at that same frequency. You can hereby exert a silent influence.

You have received an ability to create abundance in your life so as to live free and happy and to empty your cup so that it may be filled again by life and so that your awareness may expand. You have been prepared for transformation though the emergence of certain talents that are gifts from spiritual realms.

Open your heart to receive them. Let go of those beliefs and programs that limit you, of your regrets and rancors, of your schedules and your always thinking mind.

Honor your body as if it was a sacred recipe for Divine consciousness and use it to experiment higher vibrations. This glyph gives you energy, magnetic healing energy, technical intelligence, an ability to handle projects and data systems, the need to help others and the power to create harmony so that you use these abilities to express your full potential and so as to help humanity heal and evolve.

This glyph is inviting you to accept that your human form is a recipe of that same intelligence that makes galaxies move about. You are the only one who can fill your cup. Discover what truly nourishes you and what brings you joy. Don't overestimate or underestimate the strength and importance of your thinking mind but turn it into an ally and into a faithful servant.

Meditation can help you put your "always thinking mind" in the right place by becoming hollow and empty and by allowing light and inspiration ti fill you up. Transform yourself into a self-sufficient being that creates and encounters what gives him joy and what makes him happy. You can then be an intermediate between men and forces that bring progress. By serving others and life, you will find the true meaning of who you are and of your life.

Aware of how energy flows within him, of how red energy ascending from earth and white energy descending from the sky get together in his heart, the Reed uses his power to passionately explore new territories and to occupy his place in his environment. Always on the move, he adapts to the outside world and to his environment by finding the right balance between rigidity and flexibility. The Reed creates an expansion of one's horizons and awareness, both within and in the outside world. It brings an awareness of the meaning and the unity of all that is. It enables one to investigate, to master data systems existing in the surrounding environment, to awaken others by sharing information and teaching and to travel so as to explore new lands.

The Skywalker symbolizes the power to explore and conquer space, both your inner space and external space. It is capable of knowing almost everything that is occurring in its environment and to adopt a position.

He often becomes aware of what is happening before others. He is the one that reunites earth and sky, combining these energies so as to channel them in order to express what he feels passion about. The Reed knows how to break barriers, memories, beliefs, structures and judgments and as to create new paths.

He is an explorer who needs to feel free and who needs space to live and express himself. He likes to be in the outside and he loves travelling or going here and there. Lead by a strong inner fire, he easily gets obstinate and is always ready to fight to defend his ideas and principles and yet paradoxically, he is quite open-minded. He is highly emotional and he loves peace and harmony. He is always looking for something and is always willing to explore new internal or external territories.
A sleeping Skywalker suffers from his confinement into repetitive ancestral memories and patterns. He either becomes too rigid or too flexible. He easily becomes depressed and flees any serious commitment if he does not go beyond his limits.

An awakened Skywalker explores his inner space and helps others explore theirs. Amongst Skywalker people, one can find many people connected with travelling, with going abroad and with working with people in foreign lands but also many people or therapists connected with the exploration of the soul and with allowing the soul's fulfillment.

The Skywalker glyph is asking you to take great care about how you relate to space and to the outside world. Old past marks are changing and new landmarks are emerging. It is also asking to be open to opportunities and to be both well rotted in what you do while remaining flexible. That implies having bravery so as to take calculated risks.

As you flow and grow in your life, you meet unknown parts of yourself. Learn to explore these unknown parts as in these seemingly mysterious areas, every change of point of view and of vision can make you take a great lead of awareness and bring you towards what you are really looking for, i.e. freedom!

You can hereby discover the world of travelling between worlds and what is called « out of body experiences ». By changing your vision and your marks, you can turn yourself into a time and space traveler. Your most successful growth takes place where there is magic and by exploring where it is possible for you to grow, you can develop compassion for those who are also experimenting the world of matter to perfect their evolution.

How do you feel about travelling into the unknown without any guarantees? You are asked to explore what is unknown to you, what makes you feel passion and also what makes you feel fear, where your marks become blur. This part of your journey is like floating in space without the restrictions brought about by gravity. It may at first seem very strange but as you gradually get used to it, the mystery of what you find awakens deep emotions and bravery naturally emerges within you, enabling you to face every challenge and experience that comes up.

Remember that your reality only remains as it is because of your beliefs and your internal schemes that you consider as being non moving landmarks. When these landmarks change, your reality works out differently. If you root yourself in yourself, in what nourishes you and in what supports you, in what is life within you and if you connect yourself with the "Source" you will find the path that will guide you safely, whatever your destiny is. From this foundation, you can explore new mysteries and move around freely. You can they see your life as a sacred journey.

You have an incredible amount of strength and courage to explore the unknown so get access to them and feel your path flowing and you flowing along it.

One of the dark aspects of this glyph is a tendency to take a great distance from the world, like a hermit, as a reaction to the world system, to undertake some mysterious mission. Maybe you spend a lot of time alone, meditating, in artistic activities or just seeking fantasy? Maybe you find it difficult to handle daily matters? Maybe you have a tendency to flee your ancestral memories. Maybe you avoid being present in your physical body?

This can happen when you have been touched and influenced by higher expanding frequencies. The contrast between spiritual light and denser material realities can influence you to withdraw within yourself instead of expanding in the world. The solution is to become clearly aware that your soul grows through life and action in the world, when you use your different capabilities, that it then blossoms through silence and meditation and that it needs both. The solution is then to create a balance between your spiritual requirements and your daily duties, by gradually filling yourself more and more with light and by radiating that light around you so as to bring more compassion in the world.

If you feel isolated, share your love and your light through service to others. Explore the different steps of your growth by creating changes and by freeing yourself from your personal history and your family memories. Express your bravery and compassion. You are an invisible pillar who can bring paradise on this earth thanks to a balanced combination of benevolence, movement, flexibility, knowledge, communication, being well rooted and flexibility. You can hereby become free and happy and teach others how to become free and happy.

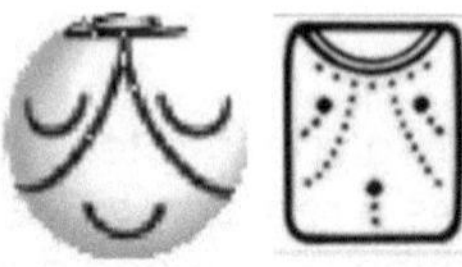

Fully connected to the present moment, the Jaguar has a multidimensional vision of reality, an inner vision, an intelligence of heart and an awareness of eternity in both space and time. He can therefore enchant reality by expressing the magic of life, of love and of love of life. He is always in motion and knows how to master and adapt in all places, in the lowlands and valleys, in the forests and in the mountains. He focuses his attention and expresses his personal power to achieve positive goals and to serve humanity.

The Magician symbolizes the strength of life and of nature, the ability to control subtle energies, the awareness of universal laws and the gift of enchanting by being magical. It represents the success of magical powers that result from a combination of a very keen sense of observation, the mastering of attention, knowledge, intuition, love, wisdom, faith, connection with the "Source" of all energy and from an ability to be in perfect harmony with the environment. It is sacredness in action.

Jaguar people have the necessary capabilities to seduce their public. They have sex appeal, charisma, strength of character, a great integrity, a strong intelligence, a very relevant and clear vision, an ability to see in the dark, a strong ability to define priorities and strong values. They live in the present moment and jump into action when the time to act has come. Quite secret and somewhat mystical, they are not always easy to grasp and to understand. Their relationships with others can be complicated as they can appear as quickly as they can disappear. They do not easily talk about themselves.

A sleeping Jaguar use their abilities for selfish purposes and their narrow-mindedness prevents them from exploring spiritual paths, other ways of life and to change their vision of who they really are. When they wake up and connect with spirituality, they can become real magicians with noble goals that go beyond personal and temporal interests. They can channel their abilities and great personal power in artistic activities like theater, dance and massage, in sports, in activities concerned with motion or vision and in any activities that require an intensive use of the body and soul in order to bring more awareness.

Their main challenge in life is to open their hearts to others and to create harmonious relationships with others. Their deepness means that the only true relationships they can create are deep and authentic relationships.

The Mayas link this glyph with the jaguar, keeper of the forests, of the lowlands and of the mountains. He symbolizes strength, power, flexibility, mobility, balance, ability to stalk and hunt a prey, permanent alertness and a solitary path. With this glyph, you can create magic where you are. You have chosen to be a seer and the Jaguar can offer you the gift of being initiated to spiritual truths.

This glyph invites you to enlarge your vision so as to express magic in your daily life, to express your powerful will in a positive way and to remain humble. It invites you to align yourself with divine will and to seek answers deep within yourself and not in the outside.

From the point of view of integrity, examine your actions, your motivations and how you use your intelligence. Through your heart, direct and align your intentions with what is appropriate. Learn to think and act with your heart, which the strength of obviousness and let yourself move in divine innocence. Be aware that these are the greatest channels of magic. Accept your power, use it to serve life and become aware that your life is living you.

Maybe you are using your power to get people's approval and recognition or to obtain a status. Be transparent and innocent! Develop your need to use your creative power! Open your heart to knowledge and go beyond your limits! Recognize your own value and be like a window through which light shines! Life will then recognize and approve what you are doing. When you are tuned into what brings you joy, you can express your beauty, your deep inner truth and you can act with integrity. Your energy then expresses much more than who you are and everything you do magically succeeds.

You can then enter in the light of real magic based on knowledge and action expressed though the heart. Use your will to express your very many qualities and talents, to follow the path that your heart shows you and to express your power to serve life. Open up to the possibility that your life can become full of magic and miracles. Connect your personality with divine will. Learn to become aligned with divine will and to produce miracles in your life and in the lives of others. By using the talents of the magician you are, you can live a very authentic life, a life that corresponds to your true desires. You can also help others do the same.

15- THE EAGLE

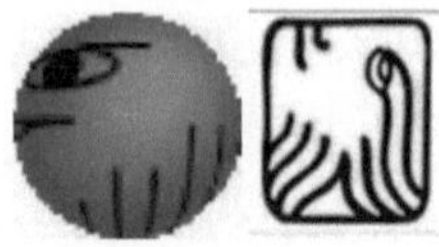

The Eagle is a messenger of awareness capable of flying high in the sky and seeing things from a great distance. He has a sharp eye and a piercing vision of reality in all its aspects. He can see things from a global point on view and easily focus on details. He uses his great power to serve life by raising people's awareness and or vibratory level and by helping them to create abundance. He knows how to place himself so as to have the correct and neat vision and he can see external things, how things move, people's paths and tracks, people's hidden intentions and what is invisible. By adjusting his vision, he can hereby bring light to every situation and seize his goals thanks to his power, his quickness and his precision.

The Eagle represents a model of divine power who serves life, who uses that power to create a better world and who brings hope and faith in life. He is an intermediate between heaven and Earth. His claws are his weapons to seize and take what must be taken. His eyes give him vision. He can anticipate events thanks to his vision of how things move and he can see every detail.

The eagle represents the power of elevation, the power to raise things up far above earthly levels, to navigate in the astral body, to look down below with wisdom and to act according to how you would like the world to be, according to an ideal, a vision and a superior awareness. This enables you to create a better world. The Eagle is the one who can oversee, supervise and guide the destinies of men while creating abundance in his own life.

You are given a superior intelligence, the intelligence of life, a strong personal power and the ability to see. You are clearly able to distinguish between solid rock paths that lead to light and those that lead into quick sands. You are able to clearly distinguish between invisible forms of life that seek to attract attention, to influence, to suck energy and to take control and true guides that offer silent inspirations and total free will.

This turns you into a responsible person. Responsibilities make you grow so if you flee responsibilities, the Eagle will track you down and seize you with his claws so as to remind you that you have been given certain talents and powers so that you use them to serve life.

The Eagle is asking you to fly along with him, to raise yourself up in the higher spheres of awareness and to remember that you have been created by the Source and that you are a child of the creator. He is asking you to look at your life and to see where you stand, where the others stand, what you have done and not done, where you want to go, where others want to go, what you can do to improve your life and the lives of those around you.

And yet he is asking you to stop comparing yourself and your life with other people and to see that your fulfillment is unique and can only be lived by you. Take some distance, observe very carefully and if necessary, change your vision or your direction, or remain on course and then help others to do so.

Awakened eagles experience fulfillment through undertaking, though trade, through service to others and by expressing information that they receive. They are independent, ambitious, demanding and tend to see the flaws or dark sides of people. Sleeping Eagles think a lot about what they could do or should do or about what is ideal but they do nothing, apart from criticizing all the time. They nourish ambitions that are beyond their abilities and exhaust themselves. They remain tied up with their ancestral memories and their fears. They remain focused on the dark side of things, on their inner struggles and on what they cannot do.

The mission of Eagle people is to create a planetary awareness by starting to raise their own awareness so that it tunes in with divine consciousness.
This requires a deep and necessary inner transformation and the development of the ability to see that positive love intensions exist behind all behavior and actions, even the negative ones.

The Eagle makes you capable of focusing on your awareness that is aware of being aware and of bringing to others the hope that their most precious dreams can come true. It gives you the energy to believe in yourself but also in your dreams and in your visions, without worrying about what other people think or want. You have the Eagle's vision so you can dance with joy in the wind current of sound and light that emerges from the luminous crystal at the center of your heart.

You are part of the global family so do your part though your path of service, by planting seeds here and there. This glyph reminds you that you are a planetary servant. Your task includes everything that makes people evolve. You are here to wake people up, to bring light, to transform people thanks to your vision, always with compassion. You are capable of making decisions by taking global consciousness into account.

Ask yourself how you can feel compassion for yourself, for your planet and for others. Ask to be guided towards doing certain types of work, relationships, places where you can live and to be directed towards projects that can help planet Earth and the people and other creatures living on it.

Allow your awareness to expand. Fly with your wings spread wide out and always seek a planetary perspective. You who can see through the Eagle's vision, you have come to bring very beautiful things on this Earth and there is a project you have come to accomplish by upraising yourself so that you can express the best of who you are.

Observe the synchronicities that come up in your life so as to find and see the keys of your destiny. Believe in your vision and set yourself in motion through action. Live by always remembering that all of us are one, as members of a same family and that when one person heals, everyone benefits from it.

Learn to balance your sense of service with correct nourishment in all domains. Follow your vision and always keep in mind the project you have come to accomplish from the divine matrix. You can hereby get access to transcendence and testify, by your vision, your heart and your ability to serve, the presence of love on Earth.

16- THE WARRIOR OR VULTURE OR CONDOR OR OWL OR BEE

By observing your inner structures with wisdom, by taking into account what your ancestors or ancestral memories have to teach you while becoming free from them and from the always thinking mind's prison, by asking the right questions, by forgiving and by expressing sacred words, the warrior can observe intensively, contemplate, connect himself with the sky, receive and share sudden inspirations, develop a piercing intelligence, become aware that he belongs to humanity and fight with bravery and boldness to live his deep inner truth. He can hereby express in matter his inner life, through action, by getting involved in undertakings or in a just cause.

The warrior represents inner strength that continuously renews itself, the power of no fear and of intuitive intelligence in action. He is capable of moving forward in difficult situations and to defend his truth. The warrior asks questions and seeks keys for his inner growth. He increases his wisdom by asking the right questions so as to increase his connection with galactic awareness.

He can question anything without fear. He symbolizes human intelligence in action and the ability to contact galactic awareness, the place of origin. He is aware of his motivations and acts according to what he believes. He is highly methodical, very disciplined and very brave.

A person who knows how to listen reaps wisdom. He has a deep awareness of the essence of all things and of the world's natural order. A person who acts with wisdom obtains results and finds a balance. Because he is connected to his own heart, he fights for causes linked with the universal heart of life. He bravely defends his family and community. He expresses himself according to inner emotional feelings of obviousness and when something is sure, he feels it neatly. The warrior is also the strength of undertaking. A warrior defines goals, an ideal, and fights to obtain victory.

An awakened Warrior fights to progress on his spiritual path He acts to protect and help his fellow men become more aware and make progress along their spiritual paths. A sleeping Warrior is afraid, asks himself no questions, totally submits to his environment, turns around in circles repeating the same patterns and continuously quarrels for material or trivial matters. Because of certain harshness, the Warrior must learn sweetness, softness, compassion and forgiveness.

One of the glyphs linked with the Warrior is the vulture and more precisely the condor. The ability of the condor to nourish himself with leftovers of dead animals and to fly extremely high up in the sky symbolizes your ability to perpetuate life from the ashes of the past, to feed on past elements to create the future, to bring what seems dead in the light of the sun so as to transform it and to bring about a renewal of life. You are a traveler who unites his heart and his mind in a state of devotion towards the divine. You seek answers to deep questions. What are you really looking for? What are you seeking? Can you see that you are seeking the roots of truth! The Warrior is the person that helps travelers cross the great river so that life can move on, so as to bring about a renewal.

This glyph brings you the gift of being capable to be an intermediate between the Divine and men. Open up to this gift because energy transmissions and knowledge are being given to you, so that you can help, without you having to do very much effort. Self confidence, will and faith are the tools of those guided by the Divine and this glyph asks you to become clearly aware of what self confidence is and to express this great quality rightly. Through self-confidence, a mystical connection is being given to you. You can claim it because it is your right to do so. If your inner voice makes you doubt, learn to take the right distance from it and to boubt about your doubts. If anger makes you furious, learn to see that anger is a disordered motion of your soul offended because it has not accepted something and learn to accept by seeing that things could not have happened any other way. You can then learn to quiet down so as to hear the subtle calls of your deep inner self. If you feel cut off from your guide or from galactic intelligence, remember that the door that opens galactic truths is inside you. Have faith in your mystical intelligence, in your strength as a Warrior and in your feelings. Claim your right to be guided and helped by efficient people. Practice meditation to strengthen your connection with the Divine and open up to become a cosmic transmitter and an agent that brings progress in people's lives.

Do what is necessary to be alive not just in your head or in your heart but with your entire being. Remember that the only real war or struggle is within yourself and that it consists in fighting defensively, by refusing and by saying "no" to whatever attempts to control you and to whatever prevents you from upraising yourself, from advancing towards more serenity and more joy and from expressing the best of who you are.. Find the right and ethical path. You can hereby encounter your powerful self and use your strength to serve others and to serve your spiritual evolution so that life continues to flow forward.

17 – THE EARTH

A feeling of unity, in a state of joy, within the body, in the present moment, between the person who knows and what is known, enables organizing intelligently and in a practical manner the natural flow of life, in harmony with the natural order of things, by following the path of least resistance. The Earth glyph represents cyclic movement, organization, adapting and evolution. It enables you to synchronize yourself with the flow of life so as to be always in the right place at the right time.

The Earth glyphs gives you a tendency to be always in motion, just as planet Earth is continuously rotating and just as natures cycles are always in motion. Your connection with Earth's natural cycles gives you a strong fertility, a lot of creative power and a deep vision of ancient wisdom. The power of Earth is also a strength of attraction, the power of gravity and the power of unconditional love that asks you to let go and to have faith as to the result of your journey.

 If you follow the pace of the always thinking mind, this glyph will give you a tendency to be continuously focused on your internal dialogue and your thoughts. Earth continuously creates new ideas and invites you to follow them. What are the new trends emerging in your life? Can you see how your path is connected to the rest of the universe? You may have a tendency to be stubborn and to refuse to let go of certain ideas!

Earth will then do its best to transform your suspicion into faith and will do what is necessary so that you can remember your path and what your true path is! Earthquakes can therefore sometimes take place within you, creating emotional explosions, crisis and major changes in your work life or in your personal life.

Earth symbolizes the power of navigation and the sense of direction, the one that follows the path of life and that naturally accepts how things evolve as a motion generated by an impulse coming from the galactic center. The Earths allows the alignment of celestial bodies while being closely connected to Mother Nature.

It symbolizes a powerful telluric force that creates movement, cycles and cohesion. If you are connected and awake, you naturally adapt to change because you deeply understand and accept that life is made of motion and of changes. You naturally accept events as they occur. You are always on the move. You use the power of attraction to attract what you need in your life. You are an intelligent, caring and thoroughful person who flows along life with great flexibility. Your reasoning abilities and your practical intelligence are highly developed. You are a realistic person who likes progress and can sometimes be interested in getting involved in social, political or spiritual communities. You are capable of finishing what you start and to materialize your goals and ideas thanks to your ability to master the world of matter.

A sleeping Earth is confined in its always thinking mind, in its stubbornness, its rigidity, its lack of flexibility and its tendency to repeat the same unproductive patterns. It resists to movement, to change and to life. It continuously quarrels with others, forgets life on Earth means living in a physical body, forgets to live, doesn't work out right and suffers from being unadapted. The Earth glyph insists of the importance of being well centered in oneself, in the heart and in the whole body, in the present moment and not just in the head. With this glyph, the Earth's gifts, like wisdom and practical intelligence are available and ready to be used. This enables you to see what is required at every moment and to act clearly.

The Earth glyph invites you to root yourself where you are, to be connected with the energy of the Earth and of nature and to listen to the information given to you through your feet. Your path should carry you within life, within matter. Find and undertake what gives you joy and seize opportunities that come up. Remember that planet Earth is turning because that is life's intention and that your life is living you, though you. What are your intentions? What is making you move? What is happening in your life right now? Can you see the connections between all this? You should because Earth allows you to see how life energy flows, the connections between things and synchronicities that occur in your life.

They are the keys to see and undertake your life projects and the mission you have chosen to undertake in life. From this vision and this state of being emerge magical things and events which help you find the keys to the tricky world you have chosen to experiment. It is very important that you learn to feel and observe the sensations in your body and to let them flow away and disappear and also to direct your attention to the different parts of your body. It is also very important for you to remember that you carry the Earth within you, that you are a member of the global family, that you only have one precious planet to live on and that you are therefore a guardian who must take care of the earthly garden which is your home.

The Earth glyph gives a tendency to think a lot and to make assumptions by interpreting what comes up. Your need to give a sense and a meaning to what comes up may lead you to reach a conclusion too quickly just because you love reaching to conclusions. Have you ever felt lost in your always thinking mind because you color and adapt the information given by your feelings, by signs, by your dreams or by a symbol so that they adjust to how you think things should be.

This tends to limit the true meaning of things. It is therefore important that you let the true meaning of the painting emerge naturally, like a landscape that gradually takes form by itself.

In your daily life, this glyph invites you to align yourself on your center, to remain focused on the present moment, to observe without making assumptions and without coming to conclusions and to remember that you have chosen to come to Earth and to experiment life in matter so as to transform yourself in order to fully express the light that can shine in the center of your heart.

18 – THE FLINT OR THE MIRROR
OR THE SACRIFICIAL KNIFE

 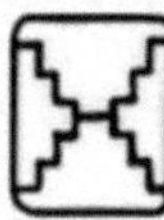

Sometimes harsh, obsessed, with a strong sense of sacrifice of what is inferior for the benefit of what is superior, the Flint is capable of seeing beyond appearance and then to slice though illusions to develop his discrimination so as to reveal to each person his reality with great precision. The Flint is aware of time's structures, of the underlying order that makes the world go round and of how things are organized. Like a building site master, he can supply great amounts of workforce and effort to do the necessary work on himself so as to get access to superior forms of awareness. His great work capabilities allow the flint to build his inner temple so as to reconnect himself with what is sacred within him and with the Galactic Source. He knows how to reflect what is but also reality's structures, like a mirror, hereby bringing many possibilities to create evolution towards ones deep inner truth.

The Mirror glyph reflects the existence of an endless divine order that is beyond time and space. It represents the power of eternity and the eternal present of all that is and of all that expresses itself in a cyclic manner.

It includes the awareness of past and future which are reflected in the present moment. It reveals how the soul wants to get access to the light of its deep inner truth and the soul's internal struggles to reunite itself under one strong will. It asks for two things, truth and order.

The flint or Mirror needs to be polished to accomplish what it is created for. To do this, he is given a sword of wisdom, an ability to perceive what is hidden, an awareness of what is true, a great determination and great organization capabilities. It can then use the knife of truth to clear up, transform and forgive but also to do the necessary work to accomplish itself.

The flint is used as a sacrificial knife. It can slice though illusions so as to get access to spirituality. It brings a discrimination that can identify, see and focus on what is negative so as to deal with it by pulling itself away from it. It can clearly distinguish between emotions and facts, between what is false and what is true. This brings him the responsibility to bring and spread out truth in this world. Truth exists in forms but above all beyond forms, within silence and action. The mirror glyph enables you to transform and get rid of decay, of stray past memories and of the small mind's fictional stories that creates drama in your life. It brings all that is to the light of truth.

The Mayas believe that this glyph allows you to see the dark side of every person, the problems they have and their bad intentions by reflecting them in a mirror made of obsidian glass.

Awakened mirror people are transparent people. They interact with others by reflecting their inner truth, without offending them or wounding them. They are slightly rebel, honest, frank, lucid and sometimes quite harsh. Thanks to their powerful organization abilities, they are capable of handling and managing complex projects, of materializing their goals and of building pyramids or great works. They also make great priest or spiritual guides. They know how to work with an extreme ability to concentrate, with joy, by doing as best as possible, as if their lives and the whole universe depended on the quality of their work. This considerably increases their personal power.

Sleeping mirror people reflect nothing or just darkness and negative things, which does not help people to grow. They often reject, condemn or abandon others because they have not forgiven themselves for having abandoned their divine spark. They can then easily confine themselves into burdensome past soul or ancestral memories that have not been transformed. They are then raw, blunt, and severe.

They lack the ability to deal with people and with form and they lack refinement and fineness. They work too much and forget to live in a state of joy.

Your mission to reflect also applies to yourself. Through meditation, you can separate truth from illusions. Illusions can then no longer be and can be put aside. This glyph's goal is, both inside you and in the external world, to create order, to set things back to order, to manifest cosmic order and truth on Earth and to do this by serving other, by serving life and by serving the world.

Your main challenge in life is to find harmony, to create harmony, within yourself and within situations that come up and then to use their power of truth and your sense of justice as a gift and not and a wounding weapon. A mirror reflects an image. What image do you give others of yourself? What image is being reflected in you? You may feel wounded by the dark aspects of certain people when they try to project their problems on you.

It is very important that you become aware that you can see how others feel and how their inner emotional state is. You must therefore learn to distinguish between yourself and others. Don't let yourself be abused and seek truth but don't be obsessed by what is correct or by what is false. Visit the hall of mirrors! See your reflection and head towards that specific part of yourself that you are always escaping from or that you cannot see clearly. Learn to contemplate the unclear parts of yourself, the ones you do not recognize, the illusions of problems. This is your opportunity to see your deep inner truth and to complete what is missing.

Look in the mirror that reveals what is in your unconscious self and contemplate those dark parts that prevent you from seeing light or that get in the way between you and light. This glyph invites you to use the world and the people around you as mirrors to discover who you are, to let things happen, to accept other people's point of view by placing yourself on the other side of the mirror and to be more flexible because if you freeze in one specific position, you prevent things from changing.

The mirror has the ability to guide you towards a more fluidic position between what seems to be extreme polarities. Judgment and acceptation are two opposite sides of the same mirror. Come in and pass through these reflections until a greater reality appears. Use discrimination to let go of any judgments about yourself or others, to push aside any doubts, any fear or any emotional problem and to make clear what is not.

Ask yourself how you support and nourish these illusions in your life. Accepting yourself as you are has the power to create inner freedom and to forgive whatever prevents you from clearly seeing who you are and the image you are reflecting. You may have a tendency to believe that your shadows or those shadows reflecting in the mirror that you perceive are so real that they prevent you from changing anything.

It is vital that you face these shadows, that you clearly look at them face to face, that you contemplate what they have to say and that you get access to the wisdom they can offer so as to get access to a superior awareness. What appears in the mirror is what you need most in order to grow and develop your potential. This glyph invites you to become aware of your potential and to express it. If you feel tied up in your "always thinking mind", in your internal dialogue and in your past history, imagine yourself going to the center of your heart and go there. Practice the art of inner silence and the art of meditation, ask for wisdom and recognize the truth when it emerges.

This glyph also suggests that you contemplate the mirrors that other people show so as to see how you contribute to maintain illusions in your life. If you have a strong reaction towards someone or something, observe it, learn to forgive and see it as a gift for growth into a wiser person. Your great work capabilities and your power to transform things can then bring to people on Earth more serenity and more wisdom.

Learn to work on yourself and to transform yourself into a luminous mirror that reflects the light of eternity. You will hereby be able to access the light in the center of yourself and also a great joy and a great inner peace.

Highly sensitive, very intuitive and strongly attracted to everything that brings greater freedom, the Storm is a catalyser and an energy accelerator. It can free anything that is confined, create upheaval, bring about spiritual evolution and trigger of healing. The Storm allows fertile rain to fall from the sky. It brings messages that create inner clarity. It can give teachings that help people transform themselves and become aware that they are part of a network and of humanity. It can help people recover their inner freedom and their right place alongside their creator.
Only a great mastering of energy and love can enable you to handle correctly the energy of the Storm glyph so as to make humanity progress.

The Storm represents the power to bring grain, source of life that allows seeds and beings to develop. It also represents the self creation of energy, a power that produces its own changes in an accelerated manner by catalyzing energy. This can create deep and violent changes, both for yourself and for the people in your surroundings. The Storm enables you to create, within you, the strength to transform, to purify and to heal.

It is an unlimited source or energy and power and it gives you the energy to do all sorts of things. Such a powerful force needs love, tenderness and vision. With these qualities, it can transform and sweep away what must be swept away as the Storm has no mercy to put you face to face with what you don't want to see and it is not always very subtle. It undertakes because it wants to purify you and to transform you.

If everything remains calm in your life, don't forget that you can also get involved in other people's storms, but the Storm always gives you the energy to see where the seeds that you can take care of are and to handle what must be handled. It also enables you to experience a feeling of warmth and safety like the one you can experience at home when there is a storm outside or in the external world.

Such energy is given to you so that you can undertake a task, a mission connected with the creation of the necessary conditions and atmosphere to produce spiritual growth.

It enables you to emotionally clean what must be cleaned and to break down mental structures and patterns so as to bring about inner clarity, freedom and renewal. It brings a universal intelligence, an ability to learn, to manage complex projects, to integrate numerous subjects and to teach what has been learned. Storm people are highly independent and often paradoxical. They are intelligent, cultured, joyful, friendly and compassionate. They love to serve. They are always seeking to experience new things. Their main difficulty is to be patient and to transform themselves inwardly through forgiveness.

Sleeping storm people generate so much energy that they remain confined psychologically in patterns that repeat themselves over and over.

They don't change and create a burdensome atmosphere wherever they are. They pile up useless knowledge, are bad tempered, often get into crisis, wound and reject other people and live in a permanent emotional storm. Such people need to find the people and teaching that will help them become free and to experiment self realization though the channeled expression of their talents. They must find the seeds and the appropriate ground that they will be able to take care of so as to nourish projects that will make them grow.

Awakened Storm people create transformations in their lives and in other people's lives. They accomplish their destiny and their life mission in full awareness. They experience self-realization and bring joy, awareness, growth, improvement and evolution in other people's lives. After the storm comes the sun, enlightment! The Storm announces times of intensive action and deep changes. It brings you to the limits of what you know about yourself and invites you to enter that special fire that transforms every level of yourself, from your foundations to your periphery.

It then helps you to go from a feeling of separation between yourself and all the rest to a feeling of unity and communion with all that surrounds you. It allows you to experience an inner revolution, to let go of old schemes, old accusations, past experiences, old memories and expectations. Life purifies and prepares your light body for renewal and rebirth. The Storm glyph invites you to go into the unknown and to cross through what seems to be a non crossable barrier so as to begin a metamorphosis. The intense feelings you have around your inner walls or barriers are in reality the fuel that will enable you to make the crossing. These feelings are your personal access to your potential and your personal power.

This glyph invites you to purify yourself with water and with sparks of light and awareness, to discover the freedom of true adventure, the freedom that personifies liberty and that can play any role, any time, without being attached. It asks you to gain confidence in the essence that brings true freedom and to be a great player if the great play of life.

You may be feeling insecure about the idea of taking risks! You are not so sure of being able to choose because you may have banged on the limit of your growth or against an invisible wall.
You may be feeling anguish. This is because every level of who you are is being transformed due to the intensive purification effect of this glyph. This means you must take very good care of your health.

The Storm glyph makes things and memories emerge from your greatest depths and from other times. It cleans up the most secret corners of yourself and reveals any separation between them and the original source of light. Because of this cleaning process, life may sometimes seem difficult and too intense and you may then sometimes desire to escape from the world's realities. This can sometimes create addiction or denial patterns, addiction to fear, sex, drugs, doubts, self depreciation, material possessions, relationships, work or too other things

In the dark side of the storm, one can sometimes feel despair and the desire to give everything up. It is essential to persevere because by doing so; you will cross a frontier that will lead you to a new unknown world, to great transformations and to the discovery of a new sacred space that is like a luminous diamond in the center of your heart. Your feelings will increase in intensity and you must let this intensity find its place within you and in your life and let yourself be carried along this intense flow of feelings. It is the energy you can use to move towards more freedom and to get access to your essence. To do this, you must move yourself, break your barriers and push aside all the doubts that make you feel separate from the Source of love and light.

This major change defies and out passes everything that exists in your reality. The Storm invites you to get rid of everything that maintains the illusion of being separate from all that surrounds you, to throw it all in the fire of the storm and your true self will emerge from ashes, purified, transformed and radiating with love. You can then use this life and renewal energy, this power of love and transformation, this ecstasy of inner freedom to serve life.

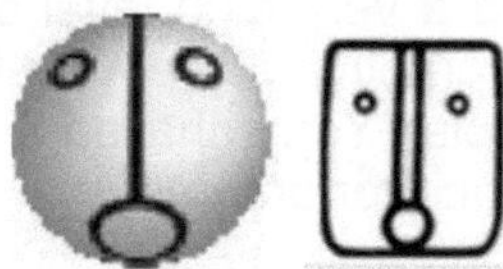

First and last glyph, the Sun symbolizes the original unit or oneness, the Source and cause of everything that is but also its culmination. Gifted with a strong ideal, with high aspirations, with a celestial vision, with a consciousness seeking to awaken, with a powerful will, with great realism, the Sun allows you to open your heart to the power of love and to see that this is what you are made of, to use your creative power, to become and to express your light and the best of yourself so as to manage with wisdom as best possible by enlightening everything that with without making any distinctions, favoritism or preferential treatments. The Sun illuminates life. It brings inner clarity, joy and fulfillment. It allows you to experiment success and to succeed your life and thus to become a testimony of its magnificence. It finally allows you to unite your awareness with the divine spark in the center of your heart and to recover your lost unity with the galactic center, with the Source where Reality originates.

The Sun is the power of universal fire. It is the light where we come from and the light where we will one day return. It is the one who illuminates and enlightens all that is by seeking and producing its own light. It is your greatest potential and the best of yourself. It represents your ability to define goals that make sense and to implement the appropriate and efficient organization so as to achieve your goals and so as to succeed.

It symbolizes the ability to control and master, creative power, the ability to handle, manage, direct, rule and govern, enlightened knowledge, integrity, solar awareness and enlightened people who generously give the best of themselves so that all potentials may blossom. Sun people are romantic visionaries and powerful centers of attraction. They love showing themselves. They can be leaders, teachers, creators or artists. They tend to be happy, benevolent, noble, and full of energy, good will, integrity and dignity. They love what has a high quality and what is beautiful.

Sleeping sun people can however be very selfish, too much focused on appearance, quite stubborn and sometimes behave like dictators. The dark side of the Sun comes from an excessive idealism, from a tendency to be blind and therefore from a tendency to confuse the world of matter with the world of spirit, not seeing that the two obey different laws. If your idealism prevents you from being realistic, adjust your awareness so as to make everything visible.

The Sun glyph invites you to accept that the world in which you are evolving has not yet reached a very high level of awareness, your level of awareness and your level of creative power and that it unfortunately is filled with very many selfish people. Your challenge is to take life with great realism without losing your superior dreams.

The dark side of the Sun glyph expresses itself when you limit yourself, when you limit the power of love and the creative power of your ideals, beliefs, principles and identification processes that maintain you in a cage and that create an illusionary feeling of separation. Observe your conceptions of the Source represented by the galactic center and of the divine spark within you.

See how your vision of things creates the world you live in and the image you have of yourself. If you are not living in unconditional love, if you do not see yourself as complete part of the Creative God of all that is and of the Source or if you over-identify yourself with your personal god, your ego, you are then experimenting the dark side of this glyph.

The shadow of the Sun glyph is love with conditions which means loving with expectations and judging others all the time. Unconditional love is a total and full acceptation of what is. Unconditional love means giving permission of each person to be and to express, without conditions, the best of who they are.

Awakened Sun people bring great warmth, enthusiasm, life and light around them. They give a positive meaning to things and are able to see beauty everywhere where it can be found. They are able to feel the great unity with all life, to help others connect with their hearts, with their power of love and with their creative power. The Sun invites you to radiate in the world with unconditional love by expressing the best of who you are.

The Sun invites you to observe how unconditional your actions are, what your expectations are and what your hidden motives are. If they are not pure and noble, it is then quite likely that you will be disappointed. What you give to life and to others will always somehow be given back to you.

Being a child of the Sun is always a great blessing. The Sun invites you to see that you are made of light and of love, that you can be a torch who can help raise many people's awareness, who can help restore love and joy brought by the use of creative power and who can help people succeed. It invites you to see that you can, if you want, be a representative on Earth of the light emitted by the Source of all life.

The Sun glyph gives you the healing power of unconditional love. It invites you to accept yourself unconditionally as you are, to act as a central sacred Sun's divine child in all your actions, to avoid any thoughts where there is no love, to radiate the presence of the solar "I AM", to remain one with the Sun's power to bring love and heat, to forgive when necessary, to free yourself and to love all human beings starting by yourself. It invites you to honor and trust the language of light within your feelings because this language is the compass that enables you to return towards to the house of your creator, deep within your heart.

It invites you to open your heart like a flower in the sun and to fill yourself with this love that creates all life with joy and that maintains the universes cohesion. You can hereby travel with your light body towards the stars where your soul comes from.

Give your permission to others so that each person can just be as they are and so that everyone expresses their creative power so that his or her potential may blossom and so that he or she may become a model of success. Learn to feel joy, to be in a state of joy, to express joy and to be unconditional with yourself as it is only this way that you can come to realize and feel that you are a child of the Sun, created by the Source of all light, which is who you are.

Practice the art of being in inner silence so as to feel in unity with what is within you and all around you and practice the art of being love and of loving with your heart. You can hereby become an expression of the divine Sun's unconditional love here on Earth.

Some more information to go a little deeper when interpreting the glyphs of the Mayan cross

The Mayas are aware that the world of matter is ruled by opposite but complementary forces. This duality can also be found in the series of twenty glyphs. The glyphs can be divided into two groups, a group that includes the glyphs 1 to 10 and a second group that includes the glyphs 10 to 20. The glyph belonging to the second group tends to be the opposite and complementary glyph of the first group having the same unit number. Together, the two glyphs become a greater whole. Each glyph needs its complementary to fully express itself. It therefore becomes interesting to interpret a glyph's complementary glyph by explaining what the situation is not and also to see if this complementary glyph exists somewhere in the Mayan cross or Evolutionary path.

1- The Dragon	11- The Monkey
2- The Wind	12- The Human
3- The Night	13- The Skywalker
4- The Seed	14- The Magician
5- The Snake	15- The Eagle.
6- The Bridge	16- The Warrior
7- The Hand	17- The Earth
8- The Star	18- The Flint or Mirror
9- The Moon	10- The Storm or Rain
10- The Dog	20- The Sun

Concerning interpretation, a glyph that is seemingly well integrated because it is located in positive positions or houses, in positions that are easily accessible to one's consciousness, like the identity position, the ally position or the origin position can mean that the complementary glyph and what it symbolizes can then be less well integrated and can cause problems, or on the contrary that it can be associated to the interpretation as a second helper.

In the same manner, a glyph located in difficult positions or houses like the antipode or occult positions can be more easily integrated by using their complementary glyphs. You can take this into account and experiment when you understand and know the Mayan cross and the different glyphs very well.

The message given by each of the 13 tones

TONE 1: Hun

ALSO CALLED MAGNETIC IN THE THIRTEEN MOON CALENDAR

The power of 1 creates a magnetic energy field around which everything gravitates, maintaining the unity of structures and defining the main goals of a person. 1 is the unity that allows things to begin, the first intention that generates creation and the impulse to start things. The vibration of tone 1 is a vibration that starts things up, of those who start new things, of independent people who open new paths like a new seed coming out of the ground.

Tone 1 or Magnetic is asking you to be connected to your essence, in the present moment, to open your heart to unconditional love and to allow yourself to express your ability to trigger of, initiate and start new events. To do this, you must be aware of your intentions and have a clear goal. You must be self-confident, listen to your feelings of obviousness and express your creative power. Just like number 1 that remains itself when multiplied by itself, you can create while remaining yourself.

You are wisdom seeking to find its path and you are even more motivated if there is a challenge. You can be a model and an example for others. You can give others the strength that helps them start their projects so that they start doing what they have come on Earth to do. Be active and express what your inner self wants to do.

Tone 1 gives you the energy you need to start what you desire, to nourish your dreams, the ones that give you enthusiasm, so that they come true, but also to help others achieve their dreams. You are hereby an instrument of the creator that is here to serve life, like a divine hand that can bring events into being and everything is possible. All you have to do is act and create.

TONE 2: Ka

ALSO CALLED LUNAR IN THE THIRTEEN MOON CALENDAR

Number 2 is born from desire. It represents a challenge, the challenge of expressing yourself within matter as a spiritual being and the challenge of succeeding to balance opposite yet complementary forces. 2 is the challenge that enables reacting. It is the awareness of duality and complementarity. Tone number two represents the complex polarity of life, the two extremes of one same energy, the opposites in form that are yet identical in essence or nature. It is spirit and matter, life and death, eternal and temporal, male and female, day and night. Number 2 shows you that reality within matter is double or dual and that everything that exists here on Earth is the result of a tension between two complementary opposites.

It makes you become aware of the separation that exists between you and the creative Source that created your spiritual body, your soul and your physical body. Number 2 is therefore a duality that triggers a reaction. It is not self sufficient and therefore leads to sharing or competing. Harmonizing this vibration means balancing extremes so as to include each one of them. If everything was all light, forms could not be seen, which is why contrast is necessary and can only exist thanks to shadows. Taking care and developing your own personal vibratory state means tuning and harmonizing your vibration with planetary, solar and galactic vibrations and including extremes that are already polarized into male and female energies.

This tone is asking you to accept and integrate the duality within you and it is likely that your life is influenced by extreme opposites. Learn to feel this polarity as a whole, where opposites are an alliance of a greater whole and the two contents of one same truth. Learn to weigh the "fors" and the "againsts", to see the two aspects of everything or situation that comes up and to take into account the female energies that unite and the male energies that separate.

Learn to live this polarity as a teaching that allows you to become free as it enables you to go back to the source of everything that is. Carefully observe what is feminine and what is masculine within you and see the role, the importance and the gifts that each polarity brings in your relationships. Pay attention to the teachings and messages that the challenges you experiment bring in your life because what you consider to be obstacles show you what you must work on so that you can move further on the path that leads you to your deep inner truth and so as to achieve what will make you blossom. The glyph existing in step 2 or house 2 needs to be embodied in full awareness and presence. It can then create form and abundance.

TONE 3: Ox

ALSO CALLED ELECTRIC IN THE THIRTEEN MOON CALENDAR

The electric energy of number 3 moves about in structured channels and carries both energy and information so as to create form according to a new idea. It enables, from the mind level, to find solutions and to remain focused on renewable service to life. Thanks to number 3, everything has its pace, its rhythm and its motion. Everything has a beginning, is born, lives, dies and becomes reborn. Electric tone 3 means movement and communication thanks to a language between two male and female polarities in the physical, emotional and spiritual levels. 3 is the tone of the saint trinity.

By seeking and creating duality and polarities, one triggers events named karmas. These are situations that one lives, experiments and then surpasses. We are born in a karmic field of action so as to learn to see life from a certain point of view and so as to serve in this world. Seeing, understanding and compensating the crack between your current state of being and the state of being where you are reunited with the Source or galactic center creates movement and action. Karma is born though ignorance. It produces ignorance and spiritual darkness.

Dharma consists of a series of actions that are in harmony with cosmic order. These actions correct and suppress the tension created by tone 2 and negativity. They create a positive field of knowledge and wisdom. They also lead to movement towards light. This corrects karma and this compensation of karma is expressed in tone 3.

Tone 3 means communication and thus listening and expressing, motion, fluidity, service to others, a flow of change and learning how to breathe correctly. You are capable of changing anything you want to change in your life. Let your creative power to transform things express itself though language, though sharing with others and through motion and then focus this energy so that you can use it to express your true desires.

Open up to all possibilities that come up so as to experiment the changes that call you, that enthusiasm you and that you wish to bring about in your life or in other people's lives if they ask for such changes.
Let yourself be carried along by new ideas and by the flow of perpetual motion and reconnect this flow of movement where it is disconnected. Through service and movement, you can express what is in your heart and you can allow others to do so too.

TONE 4: Kan

ALSO CALLED SELF-EXISTENT IN THE THIRTEEN MOON CALENDAR

Number 4 enables you to identify, measure and structure forms in life. It represents the organizing mathematical principle of both the macrocosm and the microcosm. By giving forms and structures limits and boundaries thanks to the square, it can shape things up, go beyond duality towards wholeness or self-existent forms and stabilize matter. Attention and authority are necessary to do this.

Number four represents the four elements, the four cardinal directions, the four original races on Earth (Red, Blue or brown, White and yellow), the four sides of the square and the measurement units of all material structures that are necessary to materialize form in the material world. Number four then combines with the trinity to create the seventh based structure of all life that exists.

You have within you all the qualities of the fourth vibration which are a sense of order, discipline, discrimination and alignment with life's natural cycles. You have the ability to discriminate truth from lies, to make sure everything is in its right place in time and in space, to take your place and to handle and manage your territory with caution, rigor and authority.

You can put your ideas and wishes into form, manifest your dreams or your vision and materialize in your life the vision that is inside you. You have the ability to channel your creative power in a positive manner and to build in the world your dreams and desires. You can thus serve life through your power to focus your attention on structure and organization and through your ability to work with structures and organization procedures.

TONE 5: Ho

ALSO CALLED TONAL IN THE THIRTEEN MOON CALENDAR

Number 5 symbolizes the male positive and loving polarity of the creative Source of all life and an expansion of awareness that becomes aware of being aware. It is a center with a cyclic pulsation. Every unit, however small it is, has a core or nucleus that exerts a force of attraction and gravity and a periphery where there is continuous movement. Number 5 represents that nucleus, that center. It vibrates at a certain frequency so as to be tuned in and so as to give the right tone. It is the catalyst that reveals what is without itself being altered so as to organize goals in action by dispatching the tasks and missions that need to be done. It is able to direct and manage a system's flow of energy, with will power and authority, in a specific direction but also in a circular motion all around so as to express fully its potential.

It also represents the hand and the five fingers, the five senses and the five elements that make a standing up a human being with arms and legs apart. The hand allows you to give with generosity and to receive with gratitude, to serve others and to express your creative power so as to bring about a fulfillment and a self-realization. It is an organizing intelligence capable of processing information and to apply in a practical manner the knowledge acquired.

Tone number five invites you to remember that you are the center of the universe, that you are yourself a center connected with the galactic center and that if you shift your focus and awareness to the center of your heart, where the connection with your divine spark, which is your eternal identity, is located, you will find your major task, your personal mission, the one you have chosen before coming to experiment the world of matter. Your hands will greatly help you to achieve this mission.

See that within you exists great wisdom and the ability to see truth so as to give a meaning to what is. Be simple. Be what you are and not what you believe you are or what other people would like you to be. You have the necessary authority to be a center and to express what is in your heart by using your creative power.

Having authority does not necessarily mean giving orders to others but rather it means being connected with yourself, with your divine essence and with what you love. It then means setting yourself in motion and action so as to express your potential and your creative power to go beyond the past and create something new and so as to get involved with your life, by learning to give and to receive.

TONE 6: Uak

Tone number 6 represents the rhythms that create the principle of life of humanity's collective organism. Number 6 represents the scheduling of workflow and the hexagonal ordering of cellular and crystalline structures. It acts by creating balance and its power is intelligent motion associated with efficient organization of information so that things work properly, so that life is healthy and so that things evolve towards something better and towards perfection. All structures connected with life have a tendency to achieve a relative state of balance. This enables them to reach a certain state of intermediate realization and then to continue evolving towards more developed states of being. This implies creating organized bonds and connections, data flows and sharing. Tone 6 enables the materialization of goals thanks to intelligence, thanks to a transformation of situations which occurs though leaps from one energy level to the next and thanks to a motion between a state of unstable balance to a more stable state. This implies going from one form of energy to another following a strategic action of creating a new state of balance. This creates cycles.

Nothing occurs just by chance. Every effect has its cause and every cause creates new effects, the very first cause being the Creator of the galactic center and the decision to experiment matter by moving away from the divine spark. Everything is impacted by the balancing action of humanity's collective organism. It acts by creating equilibrium, by reconciling, by moderating extremes and by equalizing so as to produce a flexible order and organization. The word organization should not here be interpreted as an everlasting order but as a transitory step to bring about growth and a gradual development of action.

You have within yourself the qualities of number 6. These are organized motion, flexibility and receptivity, the ability to react by creating balance and by increasing the state of health, hygiene, intelligence, harmony and adaptability. Number 6 gives you the awareness that there is a universal law that triggers a reaction to every action and that there is therefore a universal justice that balances everything out. It invites you go take a close look at this intelligence of life and to seek your deep self that lies beyond it. There you will find talents to bring about change in situations and relationships thanks to your intelligence and to balance the love you give and the love you receive. Once you know who you are and where you are going, you can fully express yourself in the world of matter and you can fully embody this principle of dynamic balance, of intelligent harmony in motion. You can then dance your life in a state of joy.

TONE 7: Uuk

ALSO CALLED RESONNANT IN THE THIRTEEN MOON CALENDAR

Tone 7 is a central channel that connects the first six glyphs to the last six glyphs and thus what is below to what is above. This amplifies global awareness and creates harmony in action but also paradox.

Number 7 represents the structures of the universe at the various material, emotional, mental and spiritual levels. It is divine will in action through the different levels of life and symbolizes a form of mystic power. Number seven channels spiritual energy to master the world of matter though the application of law.

World order at a material level is just a part of the global order that exists in the whole universe. By comparing the situation to the global order and its laws, one can become aware of what is right and adjust. We do not control our mind but are though by it and live in immersion with it. Mystical power is a power created by the universe and it expresses itself though the mind thanks to the power behind words. Number seven thus allows deep thinking and connection to the revelation of what is most important and to the right vision of how things should be ordered.

With number 7, you can get access to your personal connection with the source of creative power so as to express this power in matter in order to help civilization exist. You can also see this connection in every person by having a clear vision of the other within yourself, as if the other was a part of you and yet by being aware it is the other in you that you are seeing.

You have the qualities given by number seven. These are an ability to accept what is and to accept yourself as you are, mystical power, the ability to understand and unravel the mysteries of the order of life, of structures, of motion and of how people are connected. You have an ability to express your personal power in matter and to be at times always in motion and at other times in a deep meditative stillness.

Tone 7 invites you to free yourself from the need to please others and to be approved by others, to claim your mystical wisdom, to open up your heart and to align yourself with the mysterious power of 7, 7 chakras, 7 musical notes and the 7 colors of the rainbow. You can then express a power that brings evolution within matter.

TONE 8: Uaxac

This tone is called the principle of resonating octaves or the gateway that allow you to move between frequencies or realities. Just as in music, scales succeed one another in numbers of 8 steps and energy vibrates in each of the levels of manifestation, as a musical note, from the galactic center, where every vibratory level is connected to its neighbor by a vortex or passageway between levels.

Number eight allows you to become aware of the different material and energetical realities and then to make them vibrate in a coherent manner so as to shape things up. Octaves are the universe's information carriers. They enable you to get access to deep truths and to knowledge. They get their power from the great law of harmony and balance and they are the executors of this great law.

Tone 8 gives you the power to shape things in the level of intermediate worlds, between the oceans of collective unconscious worlds and the material world of three dimensional illusions, a world made of desires, fears and death. Number 8 symbolizes universal justice that checks the level of existing integrity, that harmonizes and that helps you vibrate in harmony. It brings a deep connection with the heart, with others and with knowledge of deep hidden inner truths. It symbolizes love being expressed as a flow of harmony in life according to law. It sees and re balances karmic imbalances.

Tone 8 asks you to see what is unbalanced within you or in the external world and then to act so as to rebalance, secure and to put yourself in coherence with your evolutionary path. Be aware of where your intuition leads you as it is there that you will encounter unique and highly authentic opportunities.

Seek and discover your inner harmony, the one that sounds right, by making your always thinking mind shut down and by seeking that part of you that expresses itself according to your feelings of obviousness. Get access to your deep inner truth and to your true desires, find your coherence and express the qualities of your heart and your personal power so as to shape form through action.

TONE 9: Bolon

ALSO CALLED SOLAR IN THE THIRTEEN MOON CALENDAR

Numbers 9 symbolizes the fall from paradise, paradise itself and the necessary path that returns to where we come from. Il symbolizes the materialization of life projects in the world thanks to organized action and by taking into account all information, memories and parameters existing in all the levels of space and time.

It allows having both feet well rooted on the ground while being aware of the sky above. It brings a global vision of life and can give meaning to what is thanks to an awareness of what is sacred and thanks to a special connection, though the heart, with the universe. It enables ending a cycle so as to start a new one. It creates expansion and offers the opportunity to experiment ones true desires according to a global vision and to what makes sense.

Tone number 9 is asking you to be instead of trying to be and to transform yourself into the person that makes light shine for others. You are capable of showing others the image of a new world that is open to human values and spiritual values. As you grow and evolve, you can set aside old models, based on fear and love of power, models that do not enable evolution. You become aware of great life cycles that always follow an evolutionary motion.

You can bring your inner wisdom into the real world, in time and space, in both the past, the present and the future so as to reunite your soul and your life into something complete. Tone 9 asks you to become all that you can become, to create your life in a way that makes sense so as to complete the great universal canvas, to teach others so that they can do this too and to be like a sun that shines in the world while being in its right place. In this manner you can fully express the power of your 9.

TONE 10: Lahun

Tone number 10, also called planetary, is structured energy in motion in time, both in this world and in the world of hereafter. This movement of energy expresses itself as evolution through building in every vibratory level. Number 10 measures and accompanies all movement of evolution. It transcends obstacles and guides evolutionary processes. It creates cycles of times and perpetuates itself through ancestral memories. It also builds planets and life.

You have within you the qualities of tone number 10. These are lots of potential energy, an ability to concentrate and focus attention, organization capabilities and great work capabilities, a strong feeling of being responsible, a strong motivation, an ability to build organized data systems and the power to embody your true identity separated from past memories while being able to call upon your ancestral memories.

Tone number 10 gives you the power to bring things into the real world. Your individual self can here express its true identity in connection with its essence but it is still influenced, in step number 10, by ancestral memories. This tone invites you to become aware of the memories that you carry within you and to learn how to isolate yourself from them so as to express the potential that they bring and so as to express your true identity.

On what structures and on what beliefs are your reality built? What foundations direct your choices? What are your deep roots? What would you like to materialize in your life? What are your long term goals? What is your path to get access to serenity?

Tone number 10 invites you to look deep within yourself, to clearly see your intentions and to set yourself on the path that leads you to your true essence. By materializing and by building what your heart and soul desire, you can succeed in reaching a state of serene harmony and of deep joy. As you evolve, you align yourself with the supreme model, with the world's order and everyone will then recognize your great wisdom which is your true identity and benefit from it.

TONE 11: Buluc

ALSO CALLED SPECTRAL IN THE THIRTEEN MOON CALENDAR

All structures and life itself, in its pulsating creativity always in motion, generates new realities. These realities are created by the power of word and of sound, from sounds that comes from the original sound of the universe. Continuous movement implies continuous changes, adjustments and improvements. Tone number 11 nourishes this flow of progress.

A structure that becomes disorganized into what seems to be chaos in in reality just experiencing a process of transformation towards a new order which is not yet visible from the third dimension of matter. A rigid structure that does not change is contrary to life and ends up disappearing. People however tend to seek order and safety through a standardized organization that makes one feel ok. This, from the point of view of tone number 11, is a mirage!

Most people are not aware of the huge gap that separates them from the unity with the great whole and that this gap is nourished by non evolution, by not evolving. A superior world and a superior order is waiting for us to be admitted in it. In order for this to happen, the safety of the old order must be abandoned and chocks, tremors and revelations must be experienced so as to awaken one's awareness.

Tone number 11 gives you the energy to bring about change and improvement in the way you serve and to let go of what is not useful any longer. It enables you to clean up the different layers of your personality, especially the ones that no longer serve your evolution, so as to get access to something new and so as to reach your true essence.

Tone 11 invites you to let yourself get carried away by the winds of freedom and by this liberating power so as to let go of structures, models, beliefs and images so that your real self enlightens everything that is in your environment. Closely observe and examine this liberating energy and see how it is synchronized with the flow of life.

See how it opens up a clear space where you can experiment a much greater wisdom once you cross through your limits and your resistances. Abandon what is complex to go towards what is simple and obvious. By letting your walls fall apart, you allow your real self to become enlightened and connected with the Source of all life. You can then shine like a star in the sky.

TONE 12: Lahat

ALSO CALLED CRISTAL IN THE THIRTEEN MOON CALENDAR

Tone 12 unites structures individual components into a universal whole and makes then cooperate in a fluidic manner. It symbolizes the end of a cycle, its assimilation and the pathway towards a new cycle with a new understanding of how the individual find his place within society. It also symbolizes the ability of a species to search for and reach its most perfect equilibrium and its best possible harmony. This quest for balance and evolution generates cooperation within the species.

Tone 12 invites you to turn outwards, to expand, to connect with all other human beings, to see that they are part of a single unit and to become aware that you yourself are a unit made up of lots of different parts. It then invites you to gather all the elements to your center.

If you are able to reconcile and balance, within you, the numerous polarities or elements that express themselves separately, the two aspects of one situation, of a person or of things, you will become able to unite inside you what was disunited and to get access to the totality, to the greater whole, just like a little drop of water that returns to the ocean that saw it being born becomes connected with all the other drops of water.

Tone 12 invites you to open your perceptions, to become fully aware that every part is a little bit of the great wholeness, to go beyond your usual limits by modifying your points of view, to find a deep balance within you and to celebrate everything that creates life and joy within you.

It invites you to claim wisdom, the power of faith and the ability to connect yourself with the flow of love that is all around and then to serve life and people as best you can. You can then bring your contribution to relieve people's sufferings and misery and get involved in a collective undertaking. You can hereby feel that you are a part of life and fully integrated in the eternal flow of life in harmony with universal cycles.

TONE 13: Oxlahun

ALSO CALLED COSMIC IN THE THIRTEEN MOON CALENDAR

Tone number 13 goes beyond the flow of life, of death, of creation and of destruction to fully integrate the great multidimensional universal evolution plan. It creates a transcendental vision and allows a quantic leap towards a new project which can be defined as unity with the divine spark. It offers the possibility to experience absolutely everything, to transform everything and to experiment ascension towards the reconnection with the Source of all life.

Tone 13 invites you to expand your awareness so as to include all beings on this Earth so as to share with them your knowledge, your joy and your love. Pay a careful attention to the unexpected changes that may occur in your life and in particular those that enable you to take a new direction, that bring new openings and that lead to a better situation.

Your life is made of transformations and changes. One day you are in a certain place, in a certain situation and then the situation suddenly ends and you go to another place and create a new situation. Be aware of the synchronicities and cause-effect relationships that occur and get rid of what no longer needs to be.

Remain open and flexible so as to allow changes of frequencies to take place. These can lead you towards the experience of transcendence. Don't resist to changes as they will guide you towards an expansion of your awareness where you will find peace and harmony.

Share your successes, your harmony and your inner joy with others. Allow yourself to be emotionally moved and guided by destinies hand. Move along the flow of life with fluidity and seize any opportunity that is placed in your life. You can then help the people you encounter or that come to you to advance towards their deep inner truth and bring your contribution to make people's awareness evolve.

The thirteen steps of the evolutionary path

These thirteen steps or houses are made up of the thirteen tones that we have seen previously. We tend only to consider the evolutionary path, or identity path, that is connected to the central identity glyph but we could also calculate and interpret evolutionary paths connected with the four other glyphs surrounding the central identity glyph. When we do so, we get a display as above, starting from the center. The evolutionary path of the Sun is here taken as example.

STEP 1:

The first glyph describes how you can embody the vibration of your deep inner truth, what you have come to do on planet Earth, what you have come to experiment and what your life project or mission is.

EXEMPLE: The Sun in House 1

You have come to Earth so as to embody your ideal and so as to give and express the best of who you are at every moment. You can do this thanks to your powerful will, your self-confidence, your organization and management skills, your desire to be a model for others and your ability to define clear goals and then to make your vision come true. You are here to become aware that you are light and love embodied in matter and a child of the Sun.

EXEMPLE: The Flint or mirror in house 1.

You have come to Earth so as to become aware of the world's eternal structure, order and laws, to practice discipline, to build your inner temple by actively seeking for your deep inner truth, to be a warrior capable of slicing away negative energies thanks to his ability to discriminate and also to do something with your great organizational abilities.

STEP 2:

The second glyph describes your obstacles, your challenge, what your relationships teach you and also how you can experiment pleasure, earn money and create abundance in your life.

Your challenges and your obstacles are connected to your ability to experiment the gift of just being in the present moment, in silence, in faith, in compassion, without any thoughts, in a state of letting go, while being always on the move and while finding nourishments that upraise you. You may initially have some difficulties in having faith that life will give you all you need, in seeing that there are no mistakes but just experiences and teachings and in believing that you deserve the gifts that are been given to you. You may have a tendency to give too much. You must learn to recover your true value and to express your real and personal dreams and desires. It is mainly by your own undertakings and possibly through activities connected with nourishing that you will create abundance in your life.

EXEMPLE: The Storm in house 2

Your challenges and your obstacles are here connected with a difficulty to take risks, to transform yourself, to find solutions and to heal yourself, with a fear to lose everything if you go out in the unknown, with a feeling of being separate from everything and disconnected from life, with a difficulty to use your strength and your power of transformation wisely, with a difficulty to forgive and with a difficulty to discipline yourself so as to channel your energy in a positive manner. You can create abundance through activities that require the use of psychological or technological intelligence, by being a therapist for example.

STEP 3:

The third glyph describes what motivates you to act, the energy that sets you in motion, the way you can serve others, how you can best serve humanity and the tools that can be available for you so that you can achieve your service goals.

EXEMPLE: The Wind in House 3

You can adapt and serve humanity through knowledge, trade, movement and communication, by breathing correctly so as to master your mind, through meditation which can make you feel the unity with your superior self and by using information to bring more truth in your surroundings.

EXEMPLE: The Sun in House 3.

You can adapt and serve humanity thanks to your desire and your ability to express the best of yourself at every moment, to be a model and a shining light for others, to have a vision and to materialize it, to discipline yourself though goals and actions to achieve your goals and by being aware that you are yourself light embodied in matter.

STEP 4:

The fourth glyph describes the form and the structure of your actions and spiritual path. It also describes the way you can anchor yourself in matter, materialize your life, create form and stabilize what needs to be.

You can materialize, stabilize and create form by paying a special attention to your dreams and by letting yourself be guided by your intuition, by accepting abundance in all levels of your life and by creating abundance around you, however that may be.

You can materialize, stabilize and create form through your ability to be free of thoughts and completely in the present moment, by being in silence, by having faith and compassion, by letting go and letting your life live itself through you and yet by being always in action and in motion, by finding what truly nourishes you in all domains, by flying freely in the air and also by spitting fire when it's necessary.

STEP 5:

The fifth glyph describes your main or central goal, the way in which you can trigger action through an ideal, the way you can express your authority by dominating situations that come up, the way you can give power to your inner light so that it can express itself freely and the way you can express your personal power.

Your ideal and your main goal can be achieved by learning to handle your life as a project, as if it was a seed seeking to become a tree and by acting to help beings and situations blossom to their fulfillment thanks to the use of your organization abilities.

Your ideal and your main goal can be achieved by getting access to knowledge and information, by learning to breath correctly, though trade, communication and movement and though meditation, where you can feel in unity with your superior self.

STEP 6:

The sixth glyph describes how you can adapt in a practical manner, how you can get organized for a better balance, what your rhythm is, what you are always repeating and how to find your right pace. It also describes how you can balance male and female energies to as to create paradise on Earth.

Your daily organization, your appropriate pace, what you are always repeating and your way to adapt in a practical manner are connected to your intelligence, your smartness, your playfulness and your sense of humor. Life is like a game and you just have to be careful not to loose yourself behind your different masks.

Your daily organization, your appropriate pace, what you are always repeating and your way to adapt in a practical manner are connected to your dreams, to your ability to follow your intuition, to your ability to accept abundance and to create it around you, however that may be.

STEP 7:

The seventh glyph describes how you can act in the right manner, how you can experience harmonious and balanced relationships with the universe and with people, what reveals your inner balance, how you can play your role in your civilization and how you can adjust your way of serving to match other peoples needs.

You can live a balanced relationship with the universe and with other people by exploring the unknown, by mastering the art of transformation, by connecting data, people and worlds, by using your social intelligence and by learning to see your life from the point of view of eternity which means becoming aware of life after death.

You can live a balanced relationship with the universe and with other people by seeing each one as a project, as if it was a seed seeking to become a tree and by acting to help beings and situations blossom to their fulfillment, which means using your organization abilities.

STEP 8:

The eighth glyph describes how to contact and express your true quest and your deep inner truth, how to transform yourself so as to become what you are eternally, how to create an inner harmony within yourself by putting together all the different parts of yourself, how to become one with your evolutionary plan and how to live according to what you believe.

EXEMPLE: The Hand in House 8

Here, you can do so by using your intelligence and your ability to create and use tools and techniques, by mastering the world of matter, by seeing beauty where it is, by using your two hands, though your knowledge in health and hygiene and through your ability to live in a state of grace.

EXEMPLE: The Snake in House 8

Here, you can do so by being connected to the Earth's vibrations, by seeing and handling what lies behind appearance, by transforming yourself all along your life, by learning to see and master subtle energies within your body, by doing research that leads to knowledge, by practicing "out of body" experiences so as to explore the world hereafter and by maintaining a healthy and vigorous body so that light can flow within you and through you.

STEP 9:

The ninth glyph describes how to give a spiritual or cosmic meaning to your life, how to express your inner light and how to experience fulfillment.

EXEMPLE: The Star in House 9

Here, you can do so through your awareness of beauty, your social intelligence, your relationships, your aesthetic and artistic abilities and your ability to see how things are ordered.

EXEMPLE: The Bridge in House 9

Here, you can do so by exploring the unknown, by mastering the art of transformation, thanks to your lucid social intelligence and your ability to consider your life from the perspective of eternity which means by being fully aware that there is life after death.

STEP 10:

The tenth glyph describes how you can accomplish your destiny by producing something, how you can build and materialize your life goals, how you can evolve, how you can reach your summit and how you can experience and express your self-realization.

EXEMPLE: The Moon in House 10

You will here build yourself and accomplish your destiny thanks to your emotions, by using your intuition, by becoming free from your family connections, by experimenting intimate relationships with people, by nourishing yourself and others correctly in all aspects and through the practice of meditation.

EXEMPLE: The Hand in House 10

You will hear build yourself and accomplish your destiny thanks to your intelligence, to your ability to create, to use tools and techniques, to master the world of matter, to live in a state of grace, to your ability to see beauty where it is, to handle data systems and thanks to your knowledge connected with health and hygiene.

STEP 11:

The eleventh glyph describes how you can clarify your life, how you can change it and improve it, how you can free yourself from your personal history, experience freedom and free others and what you must let go in order to express your uniqueness so as to be free and happy.

EXEMPLE: The Dog in House 11

You can here free yourself and express your uniqueness thanks to your heart, by allowing more and more love to flow in your heart, by creating special relationships and thanks to your ability to give a meaning to what you do.

EXEMPLE: The Star in House 11

You can here free yourself and express your uniqueness thanks to your social intelligence, your aesthetic and artistic abilities, your ability to see beauty where it is and thanks to your awareness of how things should be ordered.

STEP 12:

The twelfth glyph describes how you can go beyond your limits and experience renewal once you have intuitively understood and assimilated, how you can share and cooperate with the rest of humanity, how you can inspire cooperation and the powers you have to help humanity heal and progress.

EXEMPLE: The Monkey in House 12

Here, you can do so using your intelligence, your smartness, your agility and your sense of humor. Life can be seen as a game but you must be careful not to lose yourself behind your numerous masks. You will also have to channel your always thinking mind through meditation.

EXEMPLE: The Moon in House 12

Here, you can do by experimenting and mastering your emotions and your intuition, by freeing yourself from family bonds, by experimenting intimate relationships with others, by nourishing yourself and others correctly in all aspects and through the practice of meditation.

STEP 13:

The thirteenth and last glyph describes how you can out pass yourself, how to end a cycle and start a new one, how to let go of what is preventing you from experimenting your divine essence, how you can experiment transcendence and ascension, how to get access to your deep inner truth, how to root spirituality within you, how to make your happiness last and how you can spread your divine joy and your unconditional love all around.

EXEMPLE: The Human in House 13

You can here get access to your divine essence through your sense of friendship, by being a free and happy person, by freeing yourself from your past, by helping others, by serving humanity using your psychological or technological intelligence and through the practice of meditation.

EXEMPLE: The Dog in House 13

You can here get access to your divine essence by expressing the qualities of your heart, through love, by defining goals and achieving them, by creating special relationships and by using your ability to give a meaning to what you are doing.

The nine "Lords of the night's" messages

Many Mayan, Aztec or Toltec inscriptions showed the continuous and cyclic presence of 9 gods, called the lords of the night or Bolon Ti Ku. Little is known about these 9 gods. What is currently believed is that these "Lords of the night" are a part of pre-colombian American Toltec, Aztec and Mayan astrology. It is believed that they rule over invisible worlds that exist close to Earth and that humanity must overcome them to recover awareness of eternal life. Your lord of the night is like a shadow that you must integrate to recover your connection with the galactic center.

The « Lord of the night » completes the "Identity glyph" at the center of the Mayan cross and the intention of the day of birth symbolized by the tonality, from one to thirteen, linked with the identity glyph.

It helps bring some light on your unconscious self. It reveals unconscious tendencies that are active, usually against you, in certain sectors of your life. Your surroundings can often see these tendencies quite well but they may not be easily visible by your own eyes. Work on yourself and help is usually needed to deal with this dark part of yourself.

The Mayan names for the 9 Lords of the night have been lost and have not yet been recovered. They are therefore labeled by a letter and a number from 1 to 9, G1 to G9. We do however know their Aztec names.

To calculate your Lord of the night, you can search for a calculator on internet. There is one that calculates the glyphs of the traditional calendar and the Lord of the night on the following website:

http://www.xzone.com.au/maya/login.php?querystring=&ret_page=%2Fmaya%2F

Lord of the night G-1

Aztec God: Xiuhtecutli (God of Fire)
Direction: Center
Key Words: Energy and enthusiasm

This powerful god rules over fire. People born on G1 days live in the present moment and follow their heart's impulses. They are frank, straightforward and active. They love telling people what to do and tend to bring about tension and conflict. They need passion, to be active in real life and to be in the heart of events. Because they need intensity, their lives can from time to time face violent events and people.

The positive side of this Lord is an ability to be highly active, to carry a spirit of entrepreneurship, to foster enthusiasm and to be able to lead people. The dark side of this lord is a tendency to have a non controllable need to be at the center of everything and to force their views on people. They can be very selfish, wounding and sometimes tyrannical.

They are made to be leaders so they should get involved in activities where they can lead wisely so as to channel their energy and inspire other people. They should also learn to become more receptive to how other people perceive them, understand how to act according to social laws, understand the value of civilization and take care of civilization so as to avoid generating negative reactions.

Leadership and their relationship with people who symbolize authority are some of their greatest challenges. The relationship that G1 people have with their father is particularly important as more so than with other people, the father determines how G1 people will express their authority and if they will or not dare to assume leadership.

When they are able to channel their energy positively, they can achieve great deeds and lead great undertakings. Their lives can be a fantastic adventure.

Lord of the night G-2

Aztec God: Itzli (sacrificial knife)
Direction: East
Key Words: Responsibility and personal sacrifice

G2 people are very smart, clever, well organized, responsible and highly sensitive to details. They are very eager to serve and can sometimes be stubborn, obstinate and obsessed. They need to feel useful and to give a meaning to their lives.

Their lives are often centered on their work. They are very hard workers, so much so that they can have tendency to work too much and to sacrifice their private lives and their deep desires to their work, to their mission or too other people's needs.

They do not naturally go on the front stage, raise their profile or boost their visibility. Their natural reaction is to stay behind so that other people can express themselves. They never try to lead and therefore tend to seek jobs where they can serve and receive orders.

They are very pleasant and respectful. They seek harmony and have a strong social intelligence. Their main flaws are a tendency to forget themselves and to sacrifice their lives in a useless way, to not have enough awareness to see their worth and to not listen enough to their true desires.

They must learn to center their awareness in themselves, so see how precious they are and from there serve life by serving others.

Lord of the night G-3

Aztec God: Pilzintechutli (God of the Sun)
Direction: East
Key Words: Need for respect, safety and recognition

G3 people are well organized, strongly involved, highly determined, very demanding, responsible, very independent and sometimes too serious. They have great work capabilities. They are able to set long term goals and to work very hard to achieve their goals.

They grant great importance to learning and studies. They are very good at doing research and at producing written documents. They tend to want to learn things and find information by themselves rather than learn through other people and rather than ask their relationships for information.

One of their challenges in life is to master the knowledge they acquire so as to become an expert in something and a symbol of authority in a specific sector.

They need truth, respect and recognition for the quality of their work. This often leads them towards jobs that imply taking on important responsibilities. They continuously try to go one step further and to improve what exists. They need to feel recognized for the work they do but they can work very well in the shadow of someone else, of someone symbolizing authority as long as they are recognized by that person.

Their main problems come from a very strong feeling that they are not safe, from a difficulty to have confidence in their capabilities and to trust both themselves and others. They tend to judge themselves and others and to always feel guilty. They sometimes neglect form, people and human relationships which can lead to complications in their lives. Or they tend to make practical choices and to only see the practical or economical aspects of things without considering people and the consequences that what is done have on people. G3 people can thus have very strange or irrational love lives that can seem quite puzzling for people who know them.

Lord of the night G-4

Aztec God: Quintet (God of maize and feeding)
Direction: Nord
Key Words: Protection and Communication

G-4 people have a compulsive need to communicate, to spread out in space, to connect with people and to take care of people. They are jovial people who very easily adapt to almost any environment. They therefore naturally tend to express themselves in jobs connected with communication, teaching, social welfare or medical activities.

Highly emotional, they are easily anguished, nervous and agitated. They are often afraid to grow old. They need to express what they feel and talk a lot. They very strongly need to protect children and other people and need to find a healthy way to do so in order to avoid being overprotective and in order to avoid suffocating others.

Their main difficulties come from an overactive mind that takes control of their lives, from a tendency to dispersion and from a tendency to center themselves on the outside world and other people rather than in themselves.

They must therefore learn to realize the true human nature can only emerge when one stops thinking and that inner peace can only be found by going deep inside oneself. They can then become excellent caretakers of themselves and of life.

Lord of the night G-5

Aztec God: Miclantecutli (God of death)
Direction: North
Key Words: Sensibility and Susceptibility

This lord is at the center of the nine lords. G5 people are passionate and centered on themselves. They need to be recognized, enhanced, admired, to express themselves and to be on the front stage, in the heart of events. They need authenticity, to have an ideal, a high value goal and to express the best of who they are. They need to control themselves, to control people around them and events that come up in their lives.

Their difficulties mainly come from their self-importance, from their selfishness, from a tendency to be tyrannical and from a tendency to use other to achieve their goals. They need special relationships where they are the center of the world and they get 100% involved in their relationships but they tend to nourish conflicts, to try and dominate others and to take up too much space. This creates tension. They are very touchy, have a strong susceptibility and give a lot of importance to their image.

Their idealism, they quest for perfection and a difficulty to feel satisfied exposes them to disappointment and disillusionment. They can easily be afraid of being betrayed. They need to be hopeful in a more realistic way, to take other people's needs into account, to become more tolerant and to avoid blaming others for the problems they encounter in their relationships.

They do however have a very good heart. Their ability to be very generous and their commitment enables then to experience very nice relationships while their fighting spirit and their ability to handle conflicts, to have a global vision of the situation, to transform events and to handle people often leads them to occupy high social positions.

Lord of the night G-6

Aztec God: Chalchiuhtlicue (Goddess of jade water)
Direction: West
Key Words: Independence

G6 people are simple, practical, active, responsible, demanding, very independent and have a very strong need for space and freedom. They need to understand everything, to control their lives and often the lives of others too. Because they are self-sufficient and very technical, theuy often work as independent people as counselors, consultants or as an expert in some sector.

They are very demanding on the quality of their work and seek to reach a certain level of expertise and to be renown in what they do. They are also very sensitive to female values, to nature and to natural cycles of life. Well rooted in matter and often materialistic, they have a strong desire to build something and work very hard to earn money.

They are paradoxical in their relationships to others as if they love to work with others and if they need to be accepted and recognized by others, they tend to believe that their own happiness only depends on themselves and that other people bring noting but complications and insecurity.

They can thus give an impression that they give very little importance to people and that others are just there to satisfy their personal ambitions or to bring in money. That may be partly true but they do have a sincere intention to help others succeed and to bring happiness to others. When they are correctly connected to their hearts, they can become excellent craftsmen, merchants or councilors.

Lord of the night G-7

Aztec God: Tlazolteotl (Goddess of confession)
Direction: West
Key Words: Refinement and Sexuality

G7 people are focused on others, on creating social relationships and on satisfying their need to get involved within civilization. They are highly sensitive to beauty, to art and to music and are very good at understanding how the human soul works.

They need balance and harmony and they tend to flee violent situations.
They have a very strong sense of justice and a very strong moral judge.
They have natural abilities to teach, to give advice, to help other people and to work with a public.

Because they are centered on others and on their relationships, they don't always know how to listen to their own personal desires and how to manage their inner world. They may have some difficulties in handling their impulses and their sexual drives as they can easily get the impression that expressing them puts them off balance. They try to always control themselves and feel guilty when they don't. They then sometimes have a tendency to punish themselves and to sabotage their lives.

They naturally repress their impulses, sexual drives and their desires so as to avoid upsetting their social lives but from time to time, they can behave very harshly and then create major problems within their relationships.

Certain G7 people totally focus on their work, on some artistic activity or on helping others so as to channel their energy and their impulses. When they succeed in channeling their energy in a project, they are capable of great achievements. They can hereby contribute to make civilization progress.

Lord of the night G-8

Aztec God: Tepeyollotl (Jaguar god)
Direction: South
Key Words: Lucidity, movement and alertness.

G8 people are profound and complex. They are well rooted in their inner lives and have a strong personal power. They are often aware of their eternal dimension. Highly alert and very reactive, they very strongly need to express what they feel. They react very strongly, very quickly and sometimes excessively to external stimuli.

They need a lot of space, are very active and adapt quite easily to any environment. They can have a very special connection with death and with life hereafter.

They are highly sensitive and open to invisible realities but they sometimes have a tendency to focus on the negative aspect of things, on difficulties, on what's not working and on the dark side of human nature. They sometimes have a tendency to nourish negativity.

They are highly sensitive to safety issues and because they are afraid of being manipulated by others, they have some difficulties in establishing harmonious and happy relationships. They sometimes find themselves struggling with anguish and with negative thoughts which can be their own or other peoples.

Their main task is to transform their dark side, to use their great personal power to serve others and to find the path that leads them to live harmonious relationships with others, relationships based on trust and on sharing. They can channel their great deepness and lucidity in jobs connected to psychotherapy, psychology, counseling, enquiring or in activities connected to safety and security.

Lord of the night G-9

Aztec God: Tlaloc (God of rain)
Direction: South
Key Words: Independence and being self-sufficient

G9 people are very sensitive, emotional, solitary, determined and impatient. They have a very strong personality. They are very centered on themselves or on their past. They are strongly influenced by their ancestral memories and often need to do a lot of work on these memories and on their sufferings to find greater balance.

They have a strong need for tranquility and for solitude and they strongly need to experience transcendence. They have great work capabilities but they prefer working alone, being independent, self sufficient and not to owe anything to anyone.

They sometimes like to accumulate objects, usually collections or valuable objects. They are also very sensitive to nature and to oceanside where they can recharge their batteries.

Their weak point is a difficulty in establishing balanced human relationships. They also have a difficulty in asking for help and in delegating. They are so independent that their behavior can sometimes be interpreted as rejection. They have to clearly see how important civilization and social relationships are and need to develop tolerance, compassion and forgiveness. They can then greatly help others.

Astronomical explanation of the galactic cross that took place between June 1998 and December 2012

The only archeological find concerning the date of 20012 is a Mayan phrase dated from the second half of the seventh century A.D, on a monument of an archeological site, in a place called Tortuguero, in the state of Tabasco, in Mexico. The text ends by mentioning the date "4 Ahau 3 Kankin", (which corresponds to 2012 using the GMT conversion constant) says that the God «Bolonyokte» will set things in motion. This nine footed God is said to symbolize the planet Mars, the God of action but also of war.

There is however a 26800 year cycle, based on the Earth-Sun axis, that will now be explained. During this very long 26800 year cycle, an astronomical event happens twice. When it happens, it is said that great changes follow and that there is great turmoil and upheaval. To explain very simply what then takes occurs, there is a 90 degree angle between the Earth-Sun axis and the Sun-Galactic center axis.

Modern astronomy has discovered the galactic center very recently, between 1990 and 2010. It is presently located at 5 degrees in the Sagittarius constellation. For the Mayas, the Sun represents personal consciousness while the Galactic Center represents galactic consciousness and connection to the Source of all life. The Sun is "the boss" and the Galactic center" the "boss of the boss". A ninety degree angle symbolizes challenges, tension, stress, necessary changes and turmoil.

Some ignorant people came to the conclusion that it would be the end of the world! As Richard Bach beautifully said in his book "Illusions", "what the caterpillar calls the end of the world, the master calls it a butterfly". Something has been set in motion and great changes in people's awareness are starting to occur. Let's have a look at this galactic cross.

Earth-Sun axis and the 26800 years cycle

The Earth-Sun relationship occurs through a subtle balance between the Sun's gravity that attracts the Earth towards the Sun and Earths motion which maintains the Earth on its orbit.

The Earth's equator is inclined by 23.27 degrees when compared to the Sun's equator. This implies that when the Earth moves around the Sun, the Earth's equator is sometimes above the Sun's equator and sometimes below. It also implies that twice a year in the 365 day cycle, the Sun and the Earth are perfectly aligned as the two equators come to a same level during times called spring and summer Equinox. The Earth is just like a spinning top spinning around itself and turning around the sun.

It has been defined that the beginning of the « Earth rotating around the Sun" cycle begins at the spring equinox (for Earth people living in the northern hemisphere). The Earth then goes below the sun to create spring and summer in the northern hemisphere. This beginning of the cycle takes place in a specific place in the sky at a specific time. The name of the time when this happens is called "The spring equinox" and the name of the place where this happens is called the "Vernal Point".

In the west, the sky was visually cut into twelve sectors or slices or astrological signs and the Vernal point is defined as the beginning of the first sign, the sign of Aries. The Mayas knew that the Vernal point is not in the exact same place from one year to another, that it moves slightly backwards every year and that it turns around the Earth in a 25800 year cycle. This is due to the fact that the Earth also spins around itself.

The Earth spins around its axis and around the projection of the Sun's equator in 25800 years. This backward movement of the equinoxes is called the precession of the equinoxes.

Earth-Sun axis, cycle and vernal point

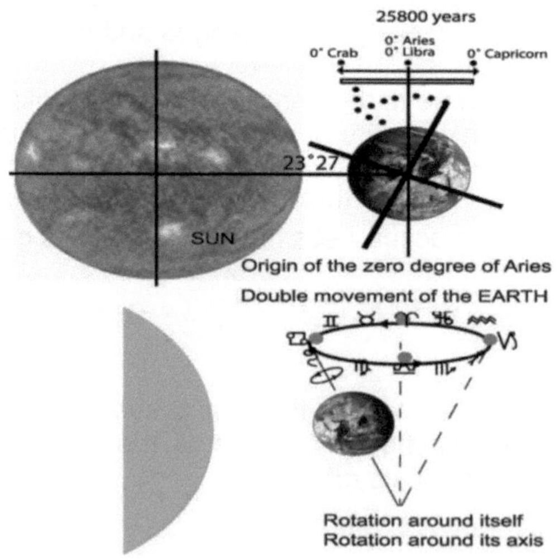

The projection of Earth's equator crosses the projection of the Sun's equator, also called the ecliptic, twice a year. The place where this occurs in spring is called the "Vernal Point". The current Vernal Point is located at 5° in the sign of Pisces. The "Reference Vernal point is located at 0° in Aries.

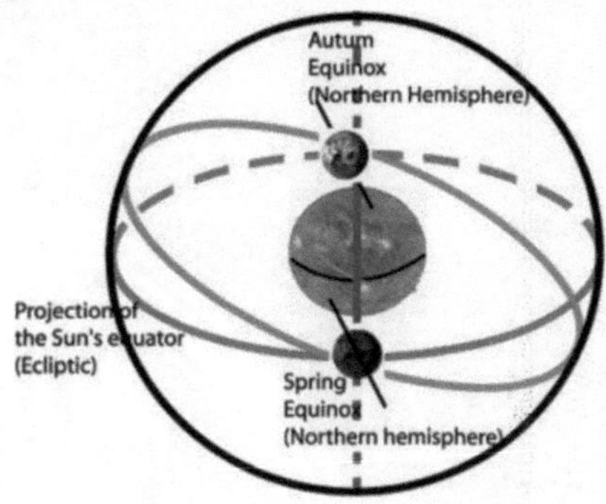

Sun - Galactic center axis.

The galaxy has a diameter of about 100 000 light years.

The distance between the Sun and the Galactic center is about 27 000 light years. The Sun is currently located about 80 light years above the true galactic center. The Sun is heading towards the north of the Galactic center and turns around it clockwise. The Sun is inclined by about 62 degrees to the galaxy's horizontal axis. The Sun is turning around the galactic center in about 240 million years

Position and direction of the Sun within the Milky Way galaxy

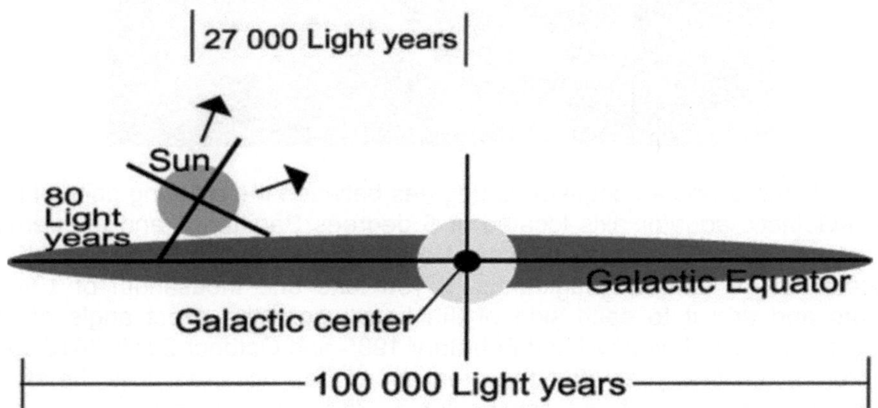

Following are several pictures showing the relationship between the Galactic axis or plane and the Sun's axis. Our whole solar system is inclined by about 62 degrees with the galactic equator.

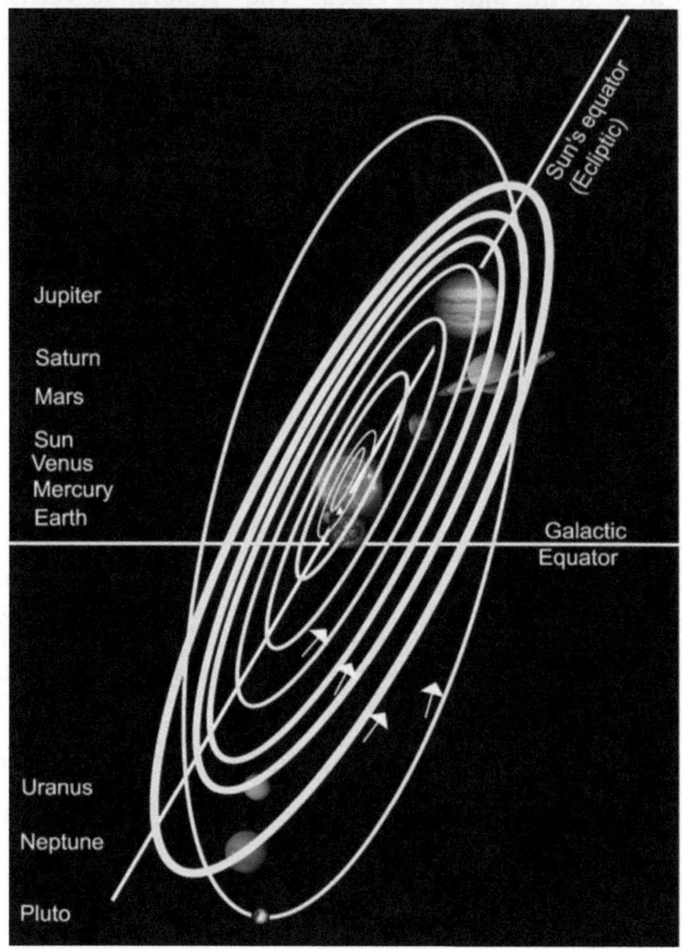

In 1998, there was an angle of 90 degrees between the crossing point of the Sun-Galactic equator axis located at 5 degrees Sagittarius and the vernal point located at 5 degrees Pisces. Note that the Galactic Center itself is located at 28 degrees Sagittarius. If you take one thousandth of 13400 years and add it to each side of the time where the exact angle of 90 degrees occurred, you will find February 1985 and October 2011. 2012 was therefore the first year after the great cross has occurred. It is therefore considered as an end and a new beginning, or the beginning of a new cycle.

You can note that every year around 20th of December, the Sun arrives at 28 degrees of Sagittarius and is therefore aligned with the Galactic center.

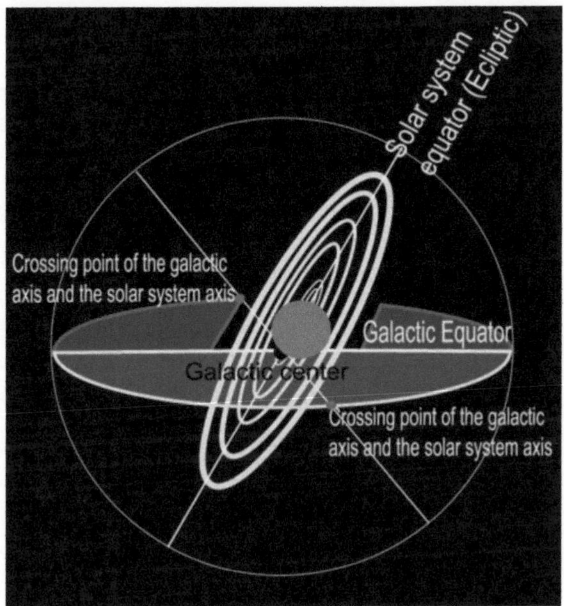

Then with the constellations (groups of stars) around the ecliptic.

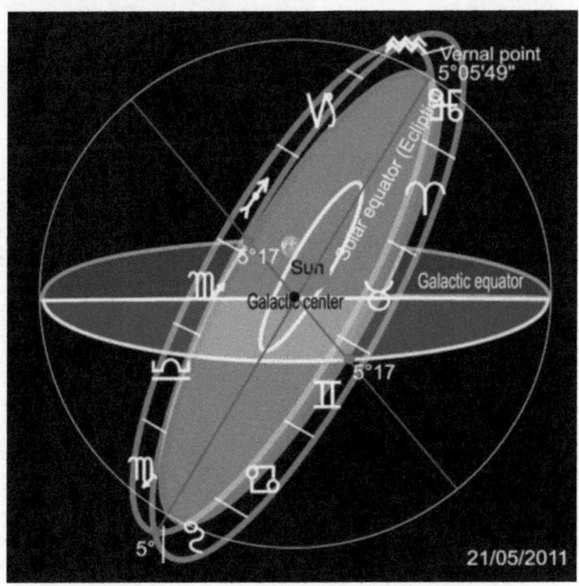

You can clearly see the galactic cross in the following two pictures

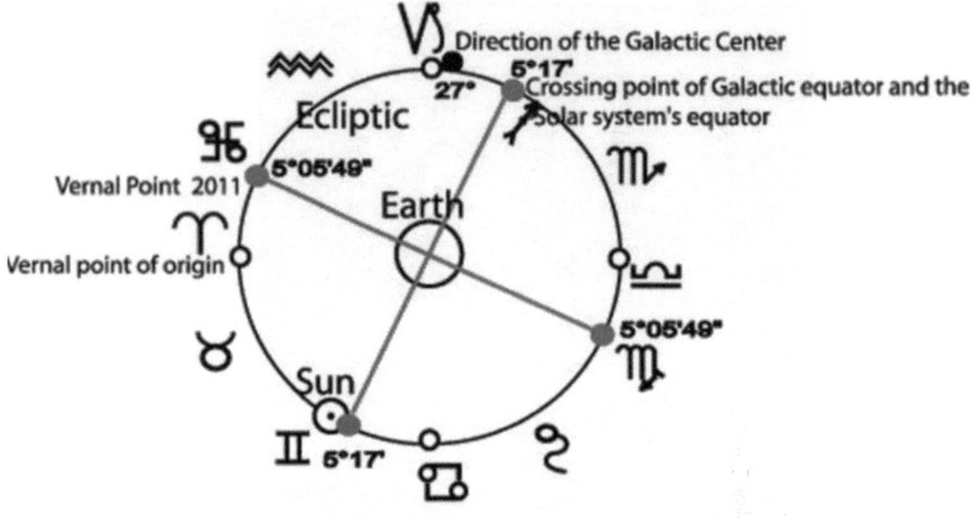

21/05/2011

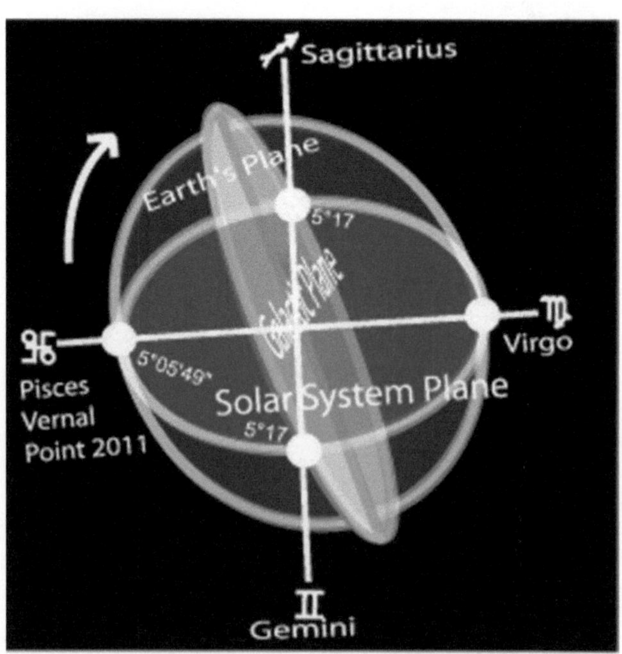

The messages passed on by Mayan sages in connection with 2012

The galactic cross increases the vibratory level of the whole solar system and therefore of the Earth. It brings about waves of consciousness or awareness and a feeling of acceleration of time. But consciousness or awareness of what?

- Of the past, of the existence of civilizations who thought they were eternal and that yet disappeared due to natural disasters but also due to disasters created by mankind when there was a wrong use of certain technologies !

- Of the existence of other planets that are inhabited by human beings, in our galaxy and elsewhere!

- Of the urgent necessity to learn to live in harmony with the form of live or the living being that planet Earth is!

- Of the fact that Humanity is one living being created by one « Source » and of the fact that human beings could live happily on planet Earth if they used their power wisely and intelligently.

- Of the necessity to give your life a spiritual direction, on a daily basis and to incorporate a spiritual evolution dimension in your life.

- Of the necessity to seek your deep inner truth (Soul plan, memories, self knowledge, self-realization, getting out of the dream, of the matrix, life after death, meditation and going back to spiritual awareness), to express your creative power and to give life the best of who you are.

Awareness of negative forces:

- Unbalanced financial system based on debts. Non productive financial system that needs to be changed. Financial logic. Control of populations by states through money and taxes.
- Control, by large firms, banks, funds, oil companies and "groups of influence" of water, energy, health, education and food industries.
- Delocalization of production plants. Economic unbalance and wide scale unemployment.
- Climatic changes.
- Destruction of the planet's forests, fishing stocks, mining resources and agricultural resources.

- Major risk that the sea level may rise between 2 meters and 60 meters in the next 200 years.
- Many resources are becoming rare (Water, petrol, raw materials and agricultural lands).
- Excess of population. Year 1000: 500 millions. Year 2012: 7 billion. Forecast year 2050: 11 billion.
- Major risks of food and water crisis ahead.
- System based on fear of death, on the need to control so as to feel safe and on a few people who live by stealing other people's energy and resources.

Awareness of positive forces:

- People are becoming more and more aware. Slow evolution of life's meaning.
- Change of vision at a collective scale.
- Environmental awareness. Rejection of genetically modified organisms and of pesticides.
- Arrival of new energies, awareness of the existence of free energy (Tesla) and of the fact that petrol can be produced by using algae.
- Development of self-knowledge tools and arrival of new therapies.
- People are getting organized in networks so as to withdraw from the existing system and create a new one. (Era or age of Aquarius).

- Collective need to create a system based on integrity, on the awareness and use of human creative power (and not the always thinking mind), on the need and ability to truly take care of people, of oneself and of others, on compassion and on the awareness of an existing universal order and spiritual laws.

Meditation of the Sun to reconnect yourself with the « Source »

Introduction: This meditation of the Sun enables you to transfer your consciousness from your physical body, where it usually is, to your spiritual body, which is located in the center of your heart. It is an action where you concentrate so as to be in silence, where you dive down to the deepest part of yourself, where you seek your spiritual body, where you observe very carefully, where you become clearly aware that you are consciousness that is conscious of itself and that you are made of a "raw material" which is love and light, where you get access to the spiritual spark of light in the center of your heart and where you become the body of this spark, of this inner sun so as to radiate within it. You hereby reconnect yourself with the "Source", with the "Source "of all life that is made of love.

Practicing this meditation is part of a certain way of life where you turn your life into a work of art, by using your abilities to serve life so as to create a better world. The keys to success are to practice regularly and to persevere. Your first goal is to reach an inner state of tranquility, of calm filled with intense life, of confidence and faith, without any agitation, desires, impatience, expectations, worries, fears, resistances nor violence.

Your second goal is to seek and search like a person who is certain to find because it knows, with the strength of obviousness, that something is waiting to be found deep inside. What is required to find it is to wipe aside what is currently covering it up and veiling it and then to calmly concentrate so as to dive inside oneself to get access to the place that is sought for. It is therefore necessary to create a space of time dedicated to your inner life, either early in the morning, before accomplishing your duties on earth, or either late in the evening, after having done your daily duties. It is necessary to have settled as best as possible all your daily life duties and worries so as to be in a state of peace.

It is then necessary to switch off your mobile phone or any noise making devices. You can start with 5 minutes per day, move on to 15 or 20 minutes, then to 30 and 45, then to an hour and then to 2 if you have the time to do so. If you have things to do after your meditation, you can use an alarm clock with a pleasant alarm but the best is to create a space of time where you have all the necessary time, without neglecting any of your duties in the world of matter. Succeeding in doing this meditation may take days, months, years or a lifetime but the reward is really really very far beyond anything you can imagine or dream of.

First step: Place yourself in a position where your physical body is completely relaxed so that you become almost unaware that your awareness is inside a physical body. The correct position is the one that is ideal for you. This can be seated on a chair, on the floor cross legged, in a half lotus position or in a lotus position is you can naturally be in such position.

This meditation requires being seated sometimes for several hours so its important that your back muscles can help you do so and to be in a good and healthy physical shape. In any case your back should be straight. When you are seated in a position that is suitable for you, allow your body to breathe naturally and deeply. Close your eyes. You can put your two hands on your legs, on your knees or join them together palms upwards.

Second step: As long as the thinking mind has not being disciplined, it expresses itself continuously, as you have noticed, by creating thoughts. The result is a continuous internal inner dialogue and a permanent inner chatter box.

This is normal, at least at a certain stage. The goal of this step is to learn to be without thoughts, in silence, without images, without sounds and to focus your attention on a part of yourself that is located deeper down that the world of thoughts.

The wrong way to reach such a state of being "without thoughts" or "without images" is to fight against these thoughts or images as this way, you only nourish them through the attention you give them. The right way to proceed is to decide that whatever thoughts or images that arrive, they are, at least while you are going your meditation, not important, a bit like advertisement boards that you sometimes see in the streets. You may see them during a very short time but you do not focus your attention on them and you just ignore them because they are not important.

When your attention is focused elsewhere, such thoughts or images gradually disappear. This is just what you are going to do, focus your attention elsewhere. At first, you can very carefully listen to your breathing and to your heart beating. You can observe very carefully if there are parts of your body that are tense and if you have any specific physical sensations. Be your consciousness that is very carefully observing and you will notice that there are no thoughts.

Third step: This step consists of continuing to observe in silence, but in focusing your attention on the energy flowing within you. It consists in entering into a state of deep silence full of life, into a vibrating silence, into an intense silence that has a sort of consistence.

Feel as if a living current full of energy was flowing through you and remain in a state of vibrant calm, relaxation and peace. Such a state of silence is similar to what you can feel if you go in the desert or if you experiment diving deep in the ocean. Continue to observe very carefully and to listen to what is happening.

You must become aware of yourself not only with your mind and with your heart but with your entire being. You need to reach a state where you feel that you are here and now, in a deep state of calm, inside yourself, in your entire body, from the tip of your toes to the top of your head, as if your consciousness existed in every part of your body as a luminous spiritual spark of awareness. You need to reach a state where you feel that you are a luminous like liquid that occupies your entire physical body, as if you where the luminous content of your physical body. The goal is here to feel that you exist through and in your entire body as a luminous being.

What you are seeking here can vibrate, either slightly or more intensively, a bit like if you were on a power plate except that it is not your physical body that is vibrating but your light body. What you are seeking has a very happy and joyous nature and if you feel joy without any specific reason, it is a very good sign, a sign that you are making progress and that your consciousness is shifting from one body to another.

Fourth step: This step consists in being in a state of firm confidence and faith, in being highly aware, conscious and alert, in diving deep within yourself and in letting yourself fall down into yourself in vacuity, a bit like a diver that lets himself sink down to the bottom of the ocean, so as to reach your spiritual body that is beyond a relatively dark and empty zone or area. You need to be like a child who knows that there is a wonderful treasure waiting to be found at the bottom of yourself. Your spiritual body, which is like a sort of crystal shaped object with almost no light flowing in it, knows that you are looking for it and it will guide you very safely. It is possible that more or less faraway colors, images, sounds coming from the invisible part of the physical body may cross through your field of awareness.

You may also have at some stage a feeling of anger or irritation or fear. It is a very good sign that you are doing deeper down. The correct attitude here is the same as what has been said before concerning thoughts, just accept what is, don't give it any attention, ignore it, don't try to fight it, don't ask it to go away, just ignore it and continue going down towards your spiritual body. If the action of ignoring such elements that arrive has no effect, it is then better to stop the meditation and to spend some time doing an intense activity in the house or in the world and to practice meditation some other day. It is only when this experience of diving deep into yourself is natural and without images or violent emotions that you can practice it correctly and safely. No image should disturb your focus. You should here remain focused on love, on finding light deep down and on joy. It is here, in this specific area, that you can experience the dissolution of emotional knots, of energy blocs, of painful emotional memories and get access to emotional freedom. This is the most difficult step for most people.

Fifth step: This step consists in placing your awareness inside your spiritual body. To do this, it is necessary to continue to dive down inside emptiness, to accept the darkness that you will meet for a certain amount of time and that for some people may be a bit frightening, to continue diving deep down more and more deeply until you feel that light is starting to appear, faraway at first and then, gradually, more and more near and more and more bright.

This light may at a certain stage look like a very bright star and this is a sigh that you are on the right path and that you must continue on that path. Little by little, a new state of awareness, full of light, love and power, becomes born within you and you within it. It is then necessary to let yourself be guided until your consciousness places itself in the center of your spiritual body.

You then become reconnected with the "Source" of all life and what is happening then become very very obvious. You then become the luminous body of the spark of light and love that is now at the center of your spiritual body. It is then necessary to abandon your will that was separated with the "Source" that created you and to immerge it in the "Source".

It is then as if you had found your true lost parents, your soul's parents and that you were once again receiving a loving hug in their loving arms. You then become a new form of life inside a new body, a form of life made of living light, joy, love and power, a form of life connected to the "Source of all life".

Sixth step: The meditation gradually ends when what you perceive gradually fades away. It is then necessary to fully accept what is happening, to return at the surface, to become aware of your physical body once more and to be full of joy and gratitude towards yourself, towards those who have helped you and towards life for the meditation experience you have created. It is then necessary to return to your daily duties.

Appendices

Table 1: Find the constant corresponding to your birth year

Years				Constant
1806	1858	1910	1962	8
1807	1859	1911	1963	113
1808	1860	1912	1964	218
1809	1861	1913	1965	63
1810	1862	1914	1966	168
1811	1863	1915	1967	13
1812	1864	1916	1968	118
1813	1865	1917	1969	223
1814	1866	1918	1970	68
1815	1867	1919	1971	173
1816	1868	1920	1972	18
1817	1869	1921	1973	123
1818	1870	1922	1974	228
1819	1871	1923	1975	73
1820	1872	1924	1976	178
1821	1873	1925	1977	23
1822	1874	1926	1978	128
1823	1875	1927	1979	233
1824	1876	1928	1980	78
1825	1877	1929	1981	183
1826	1878	1930	1982	28
1827	1879	1931	1983	133
1828	1880	1932	1984	238

Years				Constant
1829	1881	1933	1985	83
1830	1882	1934	1986	188
1831	1883	1935	1987	33
1832	1884	1936	1988	138
1833	1885	1937	1989	243
1834	1886	1938	1990	88
1835	1887	1939	1991	193
1836	1888	1940	1992	38
1837	1889	1941	1993	143
1838	1890	1942	1994	248
1839	1891	1943	1995	93
1840	1892	1944	1996	198
1841	1893	1945	1997	43
1842	1894	1946	1998	148
1843	1895	1947	1999	253
1844	1896	1948	2000	98
1845	1897	1949	2001	203
1846	1898	1950	2002	48
1847	1899	1951	2003	153
1848	1900	1952	2004	258
1849	1901	1953	2005	103
1850	1902	1954	2006	208
1851	1903	1955	2007	53
1852	1904	1956	2008	158
1853	1905	1957	2009	3
1854	1906	1958	2010	108
1855	1907	1959	2011	213
1856	1908	1960	2012	58
1857	1909	1961	2013	163

Table 2: Find the constant corresponding to your day and month of birth (day/month)

1	2	3	4	5	6
26/07 1	23/08 29	20/09 57	18/10 85	15/11 113	13/12 141
27/07 2	24/08 30	21/09 58	19/10 86	16/11 114	14/12 142
28/07 3	25/08 31	22/09 59	20/10 87	17/11 115	15/12 143
29/07 4	26/08 32	23/09 60	21/10 88	18/11 116	16/12 144
30/07 5	27/08 33	24/09 61	22/10 89	19/11 117	17/12 145
31/07 6	28/08 34	25/09 62	23/10 90	20/11 118	18/12 146
01/08 7	29/08 35	26/09 63	24/10 91	21/11 119	19/12 147
02/08 8	30/08 36	27/09 64	25/10 92	22/11 120	20/12 148
03/08 9	31/08 37	28/09 65	26/10 93	23/11 121	21/12 149
04/08 10	01/09 38	29/09 66	27/10 94	24/11 122	22/12 150
05/08 11	02/09 39	30/09 67	28/10 95	25/11 123	23/12 151
06/08 12	03/09 40	01/10 68	29/10 96	26/11 124	24/12 152
07/08 13	04/09 41	02/10 69	30/10 97	27/11 125	25/12 153
08/08 14	05/09 42	03/10 70	31/10 98	28/11 126	26/12 154
09/08 15	06/09 43	04/10 71	01/11 99	29/11 127	27/12 155

1	2	3	4	5	6
10/08 16	07/09 44	05/10 72	02/11 100	30/11 128	28/12 156
11/08 17	08/09 45	06/10 73	03/11 101	01/12 129	29/12 157
12/08 18	09/09 46	07/10 74	04/11 102	02/12 130	30/12 158
13/08 19	10/09 47	08/10 75	05/11 103	03/12 131	31/12 159
14/08 20	11/09 48	09/10 76	06/11 104	04/12 132	01/01 55
15/08 21	12/09 49	10/10 77	07/11 105	05/12 133	02/01 56
16/08 22	13/09 50	11/10 78	08/11 106	06/12 134	03/01 57
17/08 23	14/09 51	12/10 79	09/11 107	07/12 135	04/01 58
18/08 24	15/09 52	13/10 80	10/11 108	08/12 136	05/01 59
19/08 25	16/09 53	14/10 81	11/11 109	09/12 137	06/01 60
20/08 26	17/09 54	15/10 82	12/11 110	10/12 138	07/01 61
21/08 27	18/09 55	16/10 83	13/11 111	11/12 139	08/01 62
22/08 28	19/09 56	17/10 84	14/11 112	12/12 140	09/01 63

7	8	9	10	11	12	13
10/01 64	07/02 92	07/03 120	04/04 148	02/05 176	30/05 204	27/06 232
11/01 65	08/02 93	08/03 121	05/04 149	03/05 177	31/05 205	28/06 233
12/01 66	09/02 94	09/03 122	06/04 150	04/05 178	01/06 206	29/06 234
13/01 67	10/02 95	10/03 123	07/04 151	05/05 179	02/06 207	30/06 235
14/01 68	11/02 96	11/03 124	08/04 152	06/05 180	03/06 208	01/07 236
15/01 69	12/02 97	12/03 125	09/04 153	07/05 181	04/06 209	02/07 237
16/01 70	13/02 98	13/03 126	10/04 154	08/05 182	05/06 210	03/07 238
17/01 71	14/02 99	14/03 127	11/04 155	09/05 183	06/06 211	04/07 239
18/01 72	15/02 100	15/03 128	12/04 156	10/05 184	07/06 212	05/07 240
19/01 73	16/02 101	16/03 129	13/04 157	11/05 185	08/06 213	06/07 241
20/01 74	17/02 102	17/03 130	14/04 158	12/05 186	09/06 214	07/07 242
21/01 75	18/02 103	18/03 131	15/04 159	13/05 187	10/06 215	08/07 243
22/01 76	19/02 104	19/03 132	16/04 160	14/05 188	11/06 216	09/07 244
23/01 77	20/02 105	20/03 133	17/04 161	15/05 189	12/06 217	10/07 245
24/01 78	21/02 106	21/03 134	18/04 162	16/05 190	13/06 218	11/07 246
25/01 79	22/02 107	22/03 135	19/04 163	17/05 191	14/06 219	12/07 247

7	8	9	10	11	12	13
26/01 80	23/02 108	23/03 136	20/04 164	18/05 192	15/06 220	13/07 248
27/01 81	24/02 109	24/03 137	21/04 165	19/05 193	16/06 221	14/07 249
28/01 82	25/02 110	25/03 138	22/04 166	20/05 194	17/06 222	15/07 250
29/01 83	26/02 111	26/03 139	23/04 167	21/05 195	18/06 223	16/07 251
30/01 84	27/02 112	27/03 140	24/04 168	22/05 196	19/06 224	17/07 252
31/01 85	28/02 113	28/03 141	25/04 169	23/05 197	20/06 225	18/07 253
01/02 86	01/03 114	29/03 142	26/04 170	24/05 198	21/06 226	19/07 254
02/02 87	02/03 115	30/03 143	27/04 171	25/05 199	22/06 227	20/07 255
03/02 88	03/03 116	31/03 144	28/04 172	26/05 200	23/06 228	21/07 256
04/02 89	04/03 117	01/04 145	29/04 173	27/05 201	24/06 229	22/07 257
05/02 90	05/03 118	02/04 146	30/04 174	28/05 202	25/06 230	23/07 258
06/02 91	06/03 119	03/04 147	01/05 175	29/05 203	26/06 231	24/07 259
For Febuary 29th, use the same values as Febuary 28th			Day out of time			25/07 260

Table 3: Thirteen moon calendar with identity kins

The days overshadowed in dark grey and the overshadowed days in the two central columns are called « Galactic portals » and are said to be special from a vibratory point of view.

Dragon / Imix	Wind / Ik	Night / Akbal	Seed / Kan	Snake / Chicchan	Death / Cimi	Hand / Manik	Star / Lamat	Moon / Muluc	Dog / Oc
241	242	243	244	245	246	247	248	249	250
221	222	223	224	225	226	227	228	229	230
201	202	203	204	205	206	207	208	209	210
181	182	183	184	185	186	187	188	189	190
161	162	163	164	165	166	167	168	169	170
141	142	143	144	145	146	147	148	149	150
121	122	123	124	125	126	127	128	129	130
101	102	103	104	105	106	107	108	109	110
81	82	83	84	85	86	87	88	89	90
61	62	63	64	65	66	67	68	69	70
41	42	43	44	45	46	47	48	49	50
21	22	23	24	25	26	27	28	29	30
K-1	2	3	4	5	6	7	8	9	10

Monkey / Chuen	11	31	51	71	91	111	131	151	171	191	211	231	251
Human / Eb	12	32	52	72	92	112	132	152	172	192	212	232	252
Skywalker / Ben	13	33	K-53	73	93	113	133	153	173	193	213	233	253
Magician / Ix	14	34	54	74	94	114	134	154	174	194	214	234	254
Eagle / Men	15	35	55	75	95	115	135	155	175	195	215	235	255
Warrior / Cib	16	36	56	76	96	116	136	156	176	196	216	236	256
Earth / Caban	17	37	57	77	97	117	137	157	177	197	217	237	257
Mirror / Etznab	18	38	58	78	98	118	138	158	178	198	218	238	258
Storm / Cauac	19	39	59	79	99	119	139	159	179	199	219	239	259
Sun / Ahau	20	40	60	80	100	120	140	160	180	200	220	240	260

Table 4: Calculating the origin glyph

Glyph		1	2	3	4	5	6	7	8	9	10	11	12	13
Dragon		1	5	13	17	5	9	17	1	9	13	1	5	13
1-Imix		K-1	21	41	61	81	101	121	141	161	181	201	221	241
Wind		14	18	6	10	18	2	10	14	2	6	14	2	6
2-Ik		2	22	42	62	82	102	122	142	162	182	202	222	242
House		7	11	19	3	11	15	3	7	15	3	7	15	19
3-Akbal		3	23	43	63	83	103	123	143	163	183	203	223	243
Seed		20	4	12	16	4	8	16	4	8	16	20	8	12
4-Kan		4	24	44	64	84	104	124	144	164	184	204	224	244
Snake		13	17	5	9	17	5	9	17	1	9	13	1	5
5-Chicchan		5	25	45	65	85	K-105	125	145	165	185	205	225	245
Death		6	10	18	6	10	18	2	10	14	2	6	14	18
6-Cimi		6	26	46	66	86	106	126	146	166	186	206	226	246
Hand		19	7	11	19	3	11	15	3	7	15	19	7	11
7-Manik		7	27	47	67	87	107	127	147	167	187	207	227	247
Rabbit		12	20	4	12	16	4	8	16	20	8	12	20	8
8-Lamat		8	28	48	68	88	108	128	148	168	188	208	228	248
Moon		5	13	17	5	9	17	1	9	13	1	9	13	1
9-Muluc		9	29	49	69	89	109	129	149	169	189	209	229	249
Dog		18	6	10	18	2	10	14	2	10	14	2	6	14
10-Oc		10	30	50	70	90	110	130	150	170	190	210	230	250

Monkey		11	19	3	11	15	3	11	15	3	7	15	19	7
11-Chuen		11	31	51	71	91	111	131	151	171	191	211	231	251
Human		4	12	16	4	12	16	4	8	16	20	8	12	20
12-Eb		12	32	52	72	92	112	132	152	172	192	212	232	252
Skywalker		17	5	13	17	5	9	17	1	9	13	1	5	13
13-Ben		13	33	K-53	73	93	113	133	153	173	193	213	233	253
Magician		14	18	6	10	18	2	10	14	2	6	14	18	6
14-Ix		14	34	54	74	94	114	134	154	174	194	214	234	254
Eagle		7	11	19	3	11	15	3	7	15	19	7	15	19
15-Men		15	35	55	75	95	115	135	155	175	195	215	235	255
Warrior		20	4	12	16	4	8	16	20	8	16	20	8	12
16-Cib		16	36	56	76	96	116	136	156	176	196	216	236	256
Earth		13	17	5	9	17	1	9	17	1	9	13	1	5
17-Caban		17	37	57	77	97	117	137	K-157	177	197	217	237	257
Flint		19	10	6	13	7	1	8	2	9	3	10	4	11
18-Etznab		18	38	58	78	98	118	138	158	178	198	218	238	258
Storm		19	3	11	19	3	11	15	3	7	15	19	7	11
19-Cauac		19	39	59	79	99	119	139	159	179	199	219	239	259
Sun		12	20	4	12	16	4	8	16	20	8	12	20	4
20-Ahau		20	40	60	80	100	120	140	160	180	200	220	240	260

Table 5: Find the constant corresponding to your year of birth

1900	187	1952	200	2004	213
1901	292	1953	45	2005	58
1902	137	1954	150	2006	163
1903	242	1955	255	2007	268
1904	88	1956	101	2008	114
1905	193	1957	206	2009	219
1906	298	1958	51	2010	62
1907	143	1959	156	2011	169
1908	249	1960	262	2012	275
1909	94	1961	107	2013	120
1910	199	1962	212	2014	225
1911	44	1963	57	2015	70
1912	150	1964	163	2016	176
1913	255	1965	268	2017	281
1914	100	1966	113	2018	126
1915	205	1967	218	2019	231
1916	51	1968	64	2020	77
1917	156	1969	169	2021	182
1918	261	1970	274	2022	287
1919	106	1971	119	2023	132
1920	212	1972	225	2024	238
1921	57	1973	70	2025	83
1922	162	1974	175	2026	188
1923	267	1975	280	2027	293
1924	113	1976	126	2028	139
1925	218	1977	231	2029	244
1926	63	1978	76	2030	89
1927	168	1979	181	2031	194
1928	274	1980	287	2032	300
1929	119	1981	132	2033	145
1930	224	1982	237	2034	250
1931	69	1983	82	2035	*95*

1932	175	1984	188	2036	201
1933	280	1985	293	2037	206
1934	125	1986	138	2038	151
1935	230	1987	243	2039	256
1936	76	1988	89	2040	102
1937	181	1989	194	2041	207
1938	286	1990	299	2042	312
1939	131	1991	144	2043	157
1940	237	1992	250	2044	263
1941	82	1993	95	2045	108
1942	187	1994	200	2046	213
1943	292	1995	45	2047	58
1944	138	1996	151	2048	164
1945	243	1997	256	2049	269
1946	88	1998	101	2050	114
1947	193	1999	206	2051	219
1948	299	2000	52	2052	65
1949	144	2001	157	2053	170
1950	249	2002	262	2054	275
1951	94	2003	107	2055	120

Table 6: Find the constant corresponding to the day and month of birth.

Day	March	April	May	June	July	August
1	240	11	41	72	102	133
2	241	12	42	73	103	134
3	242	13	43	74	104	135
4	243	14	44	75	105	136
5	244	15	45	76	106	137
6	245	16	46	77	107	138
7	246	17	47	78	108	139
8	247	18	48	79	109	140
9	248	19	49	80	110	141
10	249	20	50	81	111	142
11	250	21	51	82	112	143
12	251	22	52	83	113	144
13	252	23	53	84	114	145
14	253	24	54	85	115	146
15	254	25	55	86	116	147
16	255	26	56	87	117	148
17	256	27	57	88	118	149
18	257	28	58	89	119	150
19	258	29	59	90	120	151
20	259	30	60	91	121	152
21	260	31	61	92	122	153
22	1	32	62	93	123	154
23	2	33	63	94	124	155
24	3	34	64	95	125	156
25	4	35	65	96	126	157
26	5	36	66	97	127	158
27	6	37	67	98	128	159
28	7	38	68	99	129	160
29	8	39	69	100	130	161
30	9	40	70	101	131	162
31	10		71		132	163

Day	September	October	November	December	January	Febuary
1	164	194	225	255	26	57
2	165	195	226	256	27	58
3	166	196	227	257	28	59
4	167	197	228	258	29	60
5	168	198	229	259	30	61
6	169	199	230	260	31	62
7	170	200	231	1	32	63
8	171	201	232	2	33	64
9	172	202	233	3	34	65
10	173	203	234	4	35	66
11	174	204	235	5	36	67
12	175	205	236	6	37	68
13	176	206	237	7	38	69
14	177	207	238	8	39	70
15	178	208	239	9	40	71
16	179	209	240	10	41	72
17	180	210	241	11	42	73
18	181	211	242	12	43	74
19	182	212	243	13	44	75
20	183	213	244	14	45	76
21	184	214	245	15	46	77
22	185	215	246	16	47	78
23	186	216	247	17	48	79
24	187	217	248	18	49	80
25	188	218	249	19	50	81
26	189	219	250	20	51	82
27	190	220	251	21	52	83
28	191	221	252	22	53	84
29	192	222	253	23	54	85
30	193	223	254	24	55	
31		224		25	56	

Table 7: Calculation with the GMT constant 584283

The names of certain glyphs are different depending on the calendar you are using.

Monkey / Chuen	Roadway / Eb	Bamboo / Ben	Jaguar / Ix	Eagle / Men	Owl / Cib	Earth / Caban	Flint / Etznab	Storm / Cauac	Sun / Ahau
241	242	243	244	245	246	247	248	249	250
221	222	223	224	225	226	227	228	229	230
201	202	203	204	205	206	207	208	209	210
181	182	183	184	185	186	187	188	189	190
161	162	163	164	165	166	167	168	169	170
141	142	143	144	145	146	147	148	149	150
121	122	123	124	125	126	127	128	129	130
101	102	103	104	105	106	107	108	109	110
81	82	83	84	85	86	87	88	89	90
61	62	63	64	65	66	67	68	69	70
41	42	43	44	45	46	47	48	49	50
21	22	23	24	25	26	27	28	29	30
K-1	2	3	4	5	6	7	8	9	10

Day sign													
Alligator Imix	11	31	51	71	91	111	131	151	171	191	211	231	251
Wind Ik	12	32	52	72	92	112	132	152	172	192	212	232	252
House Akbal	13	33	K-53	73	93	113	133	153	173	193	213	233	253
Lizard Kan	14	34	54	74	94	114	134	154	174	194	214	234	254
Snake Chicchan	15	35	55	75	95	115	135	155	175	195	215	235	255
Death Cimi	16	36	56	76	96	116	136	156	176	196	216	236	256
Deer Manik	17	37	57	77	97	117	137	157	177	197	217	237	257
Rabbit Lamat	18	38	58	78	98	118	138	158	178	198	218	238	258
Moon Muluc	19	39	59	79	99	119	139	159	179	199	219	239	259
Dog Oc	20	40	60	80	100	120	140	160	180	200	220	240	260

Table 8: Calculation with the constant 774080

The following table helps you to quickly calculate the five glyphs that make up the Mayan Cross using the constant VMR 774080. In this calendar, the day begins at midday.

1900	190	1952	203	2004	216
1901	295	1953	48	2005	61
1902	140	1954	153	2006	166
1903	245	1955	258	2007	271
1904	91	1956	104	2008	117
1905	196	1957	209	2009	222
1906	301	1958	54	2010	65
1907	146	1959	159	2011	172
1908	252	1960	265	2012	278
1909	97	1961	110	2013	123
1910	202	1962	215	2014	228
1911	47	1963	60	2015	73
1912	153	1964	166	2016	179
1913	258	1965	271	2017	284
1914	103	1966	116	2018	129
1915	208	1967	221	2019	234
1916	54	1968	67	2020	80
1917	160	1969	172	2021	185
1918	264	1970	277	2022	290
1919	110	1971	12	2023	135
1920	215	1972	228	2024	241
1921	60	1973	73	2025	86
1922	165	1974	178	2026	191
1923	270	1975	283	2027	296
1924	116	1976	129	2028	142
1925	221	1977	234	2029	247
1926	66	1978	79	2030	92
1927	171	1979	184	2031	1997
1928	177	1980	290	2032	303

1929	122	1981	135	2033	148
1930	227	1982	240	2034	153
1931	72	1983	85	2035	98
1932	178	1984	191	2036	204
1933	283	1985	296	2037	309
1934	128	1986	141	2038	154
1935	233	1987	246	2039	259
1936	79	1988	92	2040	105
1937	184	1989	197	2041	210
1938	289	1990	302	2042	315
1939	134	1991	147	2043	160
1940	240	1992	253	2044	266
1941	85	1993	98	2045	111
1942	190	1994	203	2046	216
1943	295	1995	48	2047	61
1944	141	1996	154	2048	167
1945	246	1997	259	2049	272
1946	91	1998	104	2050	117
1947	196	1999	209	2051	222
1948	302	2000	55	2052	68
1949	147	2001	160	2053	173
1950	252	2002	265	2054	278
1951	97	2003	110	2055	123

Bibliography

Ansa, Luis : Le quatrième royaume, Le relié, 1997.
Ansa, Luis : Le secret de l'aigle, Albin Michel, 2000.
Ansa, Luis : La nuit des chamanes, Le relié, 2005.
Ansa, Luis : Le mystère du Nagual, Le relié, 2010.

Castaneda, Carlos: The Teachings of Don Juan, 1968.
Castaneda, Carlos: A Separate Reality, 1971.
Castaneda, Carlos: Journey to Ixtlan, 1972.
Castaneda, Carlos: Tales of Power, 1974.
Castaneda, Carlos: The Second Ring of Power, 1977.
Castaneda, Carlos: The Eagle's Gift, 1981.
Castaneda, Carlos: The Fire From Within, 1984.

Clow, Barbara Hand: Le code maya, Alphé, 2007.

Donner-Grau, Florinda : Les portes du rêve, Alphée, 2006.

Gougaud, Henri: Les sept plumes de l'aigle, Seuil, 1995.

Ra, Bo Yin: The book of the living God, Kober press,1927.

Ruiz, Miguel: *The Four Agreements,* Amber-Allen Publishing 1997.
Ruiz, Miguel: *The Mastery of Love,* Amber-Allen Publishing, 1999.
Ruiz, Miguel: *The fifth agreement*, Amber-Allen Publishing, 2010.

Sanchez, Victor: The teachings of Don Carlos, Bear and Co, 1995.
Sanchez, Victor: The Toltec path of recapitulation, Bear and Co, 2001.

Scotfied, Bruce: How to practice Mayan Astrology, Bear and Co, 2006.

Vollemaere Antoon Leon, Apocalypse maya 2012, L. Courteau, 2009.

Personal growth services and tools

Tools to increase your Self-knowledge! To be more aware! To help give greater meaning!

Your Birth Diamond: Skype session: 1 to 2 hours.

As all human beings created by the Source, you are a beautiful Diamond that wants to shine. You can do so by becoming aware of all your facets and by expressing them in their best possible form. In this session, we will see your different facets and how you can best express them. This tool reveals your soul's evolutionary plan. It shows, amongst other things where you come from, who you are, where you are going, your challenges and your resources. It is based on numerology and astrology.

Your astral Chart: Skype session: 1 to 2 hours.

Your astral birth chart shows the structure of your soul, the experiences it has chosen to grow and its path to enlightenment. In this session, you will see the psychological and karmic aspects of your life with your schemes, your assets, your strengths and your contradictions. Your astral chart will help you understand the cause of your eventual difficulties and recurring schemes and how to handle them so that you can best express what you have in you

Your yearly astral chart: Skype session: 1 to 2 hours.

Each year (on the day of your birthday), a new astral chart arrives in your life, your annual solar chart (new ascendant sign and new planetary setouts). It describes your year's landscape, what the year has to offer, potential possibilities, opportunities and challenges. This session will help you see where you stand and how to make the best of your year.

http://www.coaching-evolution.net   06 62 51 32 26